Also by BENJAMIN R. BARBER

Totalitarianism in Perspective: Three Views with
C. J. Friedrich and M. Curtis (1969)
*Superman and Common Men: Freedom, Anarchy and
    the Revolution* (1971)
The Death of Communal Liberty (1974)

Liberating Feminism

LIBERATING FEMINISM

Benjamin R. Barber

A Continuum Book
THE SEABURY PRESS • NEW YORK

The Seabury Press
815 Second Avenue
New York, N. Y. 10017

LIBRARY OF CONGRESS CATALOGING IN PUBLICATION
DATA

Barber, Benjamin R   1939–
  Liberating feminism.

  (A Continuum book)
  Bibliography: p. 147
  1. Women's liberation movement. I. Title.
HQ1154.B29 301. 41'2 74–13887
ISBN 0–8164–9214–X

for
NAOMI

How helpless who with words alone expresses
As much of you as he can feel and see—

RAINER MARIA RILKE

Contents

Preface

To write at all requires a certain hubristic arrogance. But I have written before, and at length. To write on women requires something more: foolhardiness, sexism, bullheadedness—touched by madness enough to abandon both modesty and invulnerability. For the man who writes on women puts himself in double jeopardy: not being a woman, he must mediate the experience and reconstruct the aspirations secondhand; but being a man he can hardly pretend to the impartiality second-handedness usually provides. His account is inauthentic *and* partial, removed *and* impassioned, disembodied yet anything but disinterested. The worst of both worlds.

On the other hand, I am exculpated on the very grounds that indict me. I can plead both ignorance *and* insanity by reason of passion. I am excused, also, on more serious grounds. It is precisely the intention of this book to exhibit our ineluctable interdependence as a species: the perspective of the common human experience

justifies the attempt to bring thoughtfulness to our common human condition. I intend to provoke as disturb-
ingly as I can and will be gratified if my provocations
elicit some partial assent; some will think I should be
pleased to get out in one piece.

This is the sort of book in which the many debts ac-
cumulated make it difficult to acknowledge the few
which space and good sense permit. I have been specifically tolerated by three critics whose good will embodies
the patience of many others: Marian Wood, Lucy Behr-
man, and Erica Jong. Each has suffered my beliefs with
stunning benevolence. Richard Neuhaus and Peter
Berger nourished an early version of Section Two of the
book by taking it into *Worldview*, and Nelson Aldrich has
been a supportive well-wisher all along.

For the rest, the book speaks for itself—loudly, I hope,
if not well.

BENJAMIN R. BARBER
New York City
June, 1974

Liberating Feminism

1

Nature and Liberation
at War

WAR IS THE PROBLEM. An unreasonable war. A contrived war. An unnecessary war. Not a war between women and men, but a war between nature and liberation, between biology and self-determination, invented to reconcile men to women's aspirations—or to contain women within men's realities. A war that cannot be won but which commits both sides to spurious partisanship and fruitless combat. A war that fixes boundaries where none need exist, and reduces the integral diversity of the human predicament to disintegral polarities. A war that defines as incompatible, complementary features of the human condition necessarily intrinsic to it. A war that insists on an unreasonable choice between human anatomy and human autonomy, between roots and reason, between instincts and consciousness, between the natural past as it has formed humankind and the created future as humankind aspires to make it. A war whose only outcome can be the fragmentation of human identity.

It is not a war between the sexes, but a war between "naturalists" and "liberationists" about the sexes, for and against the sexes, for and against the bonds of nature, for and against the possibilities—the very possibility—of liberation.

War is a pungent metaphor, but look at the titles with which the liberationists have armed themselves: *Sisterhood Is Powerful* . . . one thinks at once of politics, of dominion, of something that grows out of the barrel of a gun; *Marriage Is Hell* . . . war too, one recalls, is hell; *Lesbian Nation*. . .not lesbian family, or lesbian community, but lesbian *nation* with its imperious overtones of national chauvinism; *Sexual Politics*. . . and what is war but politics carried on by other means? and, least subtle of all, *Combat in the Erogenous Zone*. . .in which war is transformed from a metaphor into an impassioned theme.

Or consider the answering volleys of adversary titles: *Sexual Suicide*. . . life, death, self-destruction; *The Manipulated Man*. . . cold war, one presumes, a "war for the hearts and minds of men"; *The Inevitability of Patriarchy* . . . as inescapable as the Third Reich, as irresistible as *Lebensraum*; and, of course, *The Prisoner of Sex*. . . wherein Norman Mailer puns his way to dazzling complacency with the initials "PW"—Prisoner of Wedlock, Prisoner of Sex, and, inevitably, Prisoner of War.

It is not simply a question of bellicose metaphors. The liberation of women appeared from the very first to be up against an implacable foe whose subjugation required total war, an overwhelming defeat. "Nature" had too powerful a past, far too awesome a record in the history of rhetorical warfare to be overcome by anything but complete victory. Hence, in the ten years since Betty Friedan wrote *The Feminine Mystique*, liberationists have waged an unrelenting campaign against nature in all its forms: against the biological roots of sexual identity and the physiological prerequisites of human reproduction; against the physical and psychological expression of these roots in sexually differentiated attitudes and behavior; against cultural and institutional manifestations of such attitudes and behavior in economic and social structure; and against political and legal prejudices supportive of these manifestations. Each maneuver, each stratagem in the campaign has demanded ideological unanimity on the inimical character of the enemy: nature as yoke, nature as ball and chain, nature as cage, nature as philosophy of oppression. What other choice is there when nature is taken to mean female vulnerability, hormonal passivity, historical dependency? When biological reproductivity is construed to prohibit psychic productivity? When procreativity is regarded as a natural surrogate for creativity?

In the wake of this reasoning has come a train of arguments parallel in form but opposite in thrust deployed on behalf of nature and against the "illusions" of liberation—the illusion of asexual personhood, the illusion that sexually differentiated men and women can ever be equal, the illusion that we can make our own destinies in the face of nature's inexorable claims. What is striking about these naturalist counteroffensives is that they have no quarrel with the liberationist understanding of nature. For them, too, nature appears as yoke, as cage, as obstacle: but as *necessary* yoke, as *comforting* cage, as *immovable* obstacle. Naturalists do not exactly want to crawl back into the womb, they simply deny that anybody can ever crawl out of it. They do not necessarily applaud female passivity, they declare it an unavoidable fact. Thus, there is a startling convergence among liberationists and naturalists: they face one another as advocates and adversaries across a single barricade labeled "nature," liberationists trying to escape up and over a wall of debris they believe has been thrown up by their enemies, naturalists pushing them back down with the cry, "Natural! These walls are natural! They are extensions of your own bodies from which there can be no escape." There is no disagreement, only antipathy, no uncertainty about issues, only opposition.

"The barricades you would breach are superstructures of your own anatomy," shout the neo-Freudian defenders of the natural order, "and anatomy is destiny."

"That may well be," concurs Shulamith Firestone from the other side of the rubble, "but then To Hell With Anatomy! Up With Androgyny!"

"Without you we are impotent sticks," warns Norman Mailer, "and without us you are empty holes."

"Then we shall fill the holes with dildoes and make sticks of our clitorises and with the help of digits be men to ourselves." Jill Johnston is speaking.

"Do what you will with your clitorises," retorts George Gilder, "you cannot transform your wombs."

"If we must, we will rip them out!" comes the answer.

The rhetoric is escalating. There is no such thing as limited war.

"What about the children?"

"Artificial insemination! Extra-uteral gestation!"

"You'll still need our semen."

"Test-tubes! Clones! We've got the hardware!"

"Who will raise them?"

"They will be liberated too! They can raise themselves."

Mailer senses they are skirmishing on the enemy's turf. You can't outbitch a woman. He shifts ground: "What about sexuality? Sensuality?" And then, the clincher: *"Tenderness?"*

"Politics," replies Kate Millet instantly, "it's all politics."

"Politics?" Mailer answers wondrously. "The cosmic orgasm is only. . ."

"Politics!" interrupts Steven Goldberg, urging Mailer to give him a little room. "It *is* all politics. Which is exactly why patriarchy is inevitable. Sex is political means politics is sexual."

"That's *my* argument," exclaims Millet.

"No, mine," screams Goldberg. "The natural laws of paternity justify the social laws of patriarchy. That is sexual politics."

"Then destroy paternity! Annihilate sexuality." Firestone believes in logical consistency, if she believes in anything.

"What," reply a chorus of naturalists, "are you deaf? You can't move the immovable! Or resist the irresistible! Would you liberate us from gravitation?"

"Airplanes! Balloons! What do you think liberation means?"

"We're men, not machines!"

"We'll fix that!" cries Firestone, the victory momentarily hers.

In the din of this discordant unanimity, the meaning of both nature and liberation is lost. Phrase-mongers and munitions makers are rarely prudent wordsmiths, especially when it suits both sides to use weapons of a commonly perverse caliber. Those who enter the fray find themselves committed to a verbal weaponry that predetermines which battles they will fight, and how. They may choose sides, but not issues. Which is what makes the war so unreasonable, so endlessly fruitless, so unnecessary. How can there be consolation in the victory of either of the antagonists, when neither seems able to understand our species' integral character? The war on nature is being waged by well-intended liberationists who not only suffer from a stunning indifference to the character of their foe, but who seriously misperceive the liberty in whose name they do battle. That liberty probably loses its meaning apart from human purpose, human need, and human sexuality as determined at least in part by biology and physiology—that is to say, by nature itself—is an insight warriors assaulting nature's own fortress cannot permit themselves.

The war against liberation is, in the same fashion, in the hands of naturalists who are not only amazingly oblivious to the possibilities of creative self-definition and equitable personhood that enrich and complement our sexual identities, but who seem terribly murky about the idea of nature in whose hallowed name they have launched their redoubtable counteroffensive. That nature is a beginning point but hardly the end point of humankind's collective identity suggests a geography that can only confuse those bearing the standard of ethology back into our species' animal past.

In short, the liberationists seem to understand far too little about liberty and its meaning as an integral aspect of human nature, while the naturalists understand still less about nature and its meaning as a context for liberation. In their common misunderstanding, however, the two understand one another very well—and so the battle between them rages on, intensely, inconclusively, unproductively.

I write to offer an alternative to war, to give substance to the position of non-belligerents impressed by the claims of nature but drawn too by the aspirations of liberation. I write because I cannot accept the terms of war. I refuse to acknowledge that to be free we must surrender our heterosexuality and the complementarity it entails; or that human nature is inimical to human freedom. I suspect that our choices are a great deal more profound than the naturalists realize, yet far less arbitrary and independent of nature than liberationists hope. I am not satisfied with the status quo or its complacent defenders' appeals to our animal origins, yet I cannot feel persuaded by a liberationist program for change that requires us to surrender our nature to secure our freedom. There is another, a different way of looking at the issue of woman's place and man's place in their common world. Before subjecting the liberationists and their adversaries to a more searching inquiry in the next two sections, I want to convey the spirit of this alternative perspective. For it underlies all of the criticism that follows and generates the approach to peace terms and a practical program that concludes the book.

When naturalists and liberationists look at the conditions of human existence either to underscore their inevitability or to impeach their desirability, they are diverted by what I would like to call the animal and the divine elements in humankind. Women and men are undeniably if not inalterably animals—living organisms bound by the laws of birth and death, growth and decay, desire and aversion that are common to all animals. The animal in our nature suggests a degree of biological determinism, of inescapable necessity, in the human mode of being from which ethologists and naturalists both draw their succor and launch their arguments. So powerful is this animality that certain liberationists have recently assayed to deflect the necessitarian argument to their own purposes, arguing, as Elaine Morgan has, that evolution has followed the path of female rather than male animality, or, as Mary Jane Sherfey has, that sexual superiority lies with the female's capacity for endless orgasm rather than with the males's vastly overrated libido. Lulling naturalists into complacency by acknowledging that anatomy is indeed destiny, they quickly dispatch them by demonstrating that female anatomy is "naturally" superior. To liberate women is simply to restore them to their natural superiority. Esther Vilar's *The Manipulated Man*, the subject of a more extensive review further on, can be seen here as a variation on this inverted naturalism: woman is a particularly vile and manipulative genus of the human species. She enslaves her masculine counterpart even as she persuades him—in his infinite gullibility—that he is her master.

But for the most part, liberationists dwell on the other side of our condition, underplaying the role of biological animalism while focusing on the potential capacity for transcendent personhood, for creative self-definition, for making our own destinies despite the constraints of nature. They regard humans as capable of, in the broadest figurative sense, divinity—possessed of the knowledge, the power, and the freedom of gods to make over themselves and their world in their own self-chosen image. From this comes the raucous battle of naturalists and liberationists, the former insisting we are finally animals however much we wish to be gods, the latter certain we are gods if only by the eloquence with which we insist we are animals.

There are, of course, varying degrees of hardness and softness among proponents of the two extremes. The soft determinists on the side of animality concede that humans are a rather peculiar kind of animal, possessed of a possibly unique capacity for language, reason and civilization. (However, this breed of naturalist is always on the lookout for signs indicating that lions "socialize," dolphins "communicate," apes use "tools," and computer-equipped chimpanzees "symbolize" in humanly intelligible ways—presumably to prove that we are animals no matter what we do.) To these observers, our institutions always bear the imprint of our animality, either as vehicles through which animal desire is channeled and accommodated in multi-person (social) settings, or as repressive instruments of self-preservation designed by the prudence of a species that understands how inimical to survival its own animal nature can be. In other words, whether civilization tames sexuality in the name of species survival, as Freud and his latest naturalist disciple George Gilder assert, or merely engineers the wherewithal of its expression, as patriarchalists such as Steven Goldberg would have us believe, it is always—in the naturalist perspective—in the service of the animal in humankind.

Soft liberationists, realists we might say, also acknowledge that civilization plays a role. It is, after all, difficult to imagine how we might remake our destinies in a total vacuum unconstrained by the forms of society and the substantive norms of our culture. We may, however, continue to regard civilization as potentially expressive of our aspirations to divinity. Unlike nature, artificial institutions are presumably vulnerable to manipulation and reform; unlike nature, they enslave us only to the degree we choose to be enslaved. The claim that sexual inequality is culture-based rather than purely natural is thus a particular feature of liberationist appeals to sociology. It is easier to beat society than nature: and to the extent it can be shown that society is the culprit, whatever reforms nature might resist are rendered feasible. It makes more sense to annihilate the transient forms of culture than the permanent structures of some putative human nature—although ultimately, malleable institutions are deemed products of immalleable nature by the not-altogether-consistent liberationist logic.

Superficially, there appears to be a confusing overlap between soft naturalists and realistic liberationists in their common focus on the uses and abuses of civilization. A more careful look reveals that among naturalists civilization is generally but a disguise for nature (whether repressive or expressive), whereas among liberationists it is almost always a cloak for our aspirations— less realized at some times than others, but always an instrument of conscious liberation, or conscious oppression.

It is my belief that neither of these positions, even in their compromised soft forms, provides a satisfactory understanding of human nature or human liberation. Surely Aristotle was closer to the truth when he suggested that to be human is precisely to be neither animal nor divine but somewhere between in that paradox-strewn realm where the animal and the divine converge to create a species of beings *sui generis.* If we are creatures of animal necessity, our necessity impels us to freedom in a manner compromising to our animality. If our destiny is rooted in biology it reaches towards transcendence, much as a tree draws nourishment from the earth for its flight to the sky, never quite getting aloft but soaring above the earthworm for all that. If desire reflects animal needs, the power of consciousness to defer, thwart or direct desire promotes liberation from animal needs.

Yet by the same token, the realization of the autonomous self associated with liberation (properly understood) presupposes a convincing image of self rooted in something less arbitrary than random self-creation, rooted in other words in the animal natures with which we are born. Transcendence is possible only when the transcendor survives in some recognizable form. In fulfilling our ends we actualize that which, in some significant sense, is already present in us. The aspiration to eternity associated with the highest forms of consciousness is endowed with poignancy by the inevitability of death for the life system that supports consciousness.

Aristotle, the probably apocryphal story goes, would grasp a handful of brass balls poised over a tin bowl when retiring; should he be lulled by his body into sleep the clatter of the dropped spheres would recall his "dead" soul to consciousness; retrieving the balls, he would renew his struggle with mortality. What a fearful tribute to the dialectic of the animal and the divine in our natures—as well as to the human impulse to risk self-provoked madness in pursuit of divinity (divinity itself being a kind of madness in the eyes of the ancients). Animals have no fear of sleep, gods no need of it. We poor humans sleep fitfully, our hands clutching desperately for a perfection our mortality will not let us claim.

These poignant dialectics go unnoticed, however, by nature's liberationist assailants and its embattled defenders. The assumption among the warriors is that we are either animals—period; or gods—period; when in fact we are merely human: animal-rooted, god-aspiring, bound by nature, bound for liberation. Liberationists and naturalists alike see in nature a tyranny that either prohibits (naturalists) or enjoins (liberationists) emancipation. It may manifest itself as the yoke of natural scarcity (Hobbes or Marx), or as libidinal determinism (Freud), but it always appears as the enemy of liberty. Yet from the dialectical perspective, liberty is possible only in the context of some notion of the natural, just as self-liberation is meaningful only in the context of some rooted notion of the self. Roots are not chains, and if biological arguments were not so often advanced with the aid of mechanistic metaphors this might be more apparent to naturalists. Flowers severed from their roots are not liberated but killed. One of the great fallacies of the liberationists, explored at length in the fourth section of this book, is that deracination means liberation, that to be uprooted and to be free are the same thing. They surely are not. When Rousseau opens his greatest political treatise with the words "men are born free, yet everywhere they are in chains," he suggests that freedom is an aspect of realizing our nature, not a means of its denial.

If liberationists forget the roots of liberty, naturalists too often overlook the liberating potential of roots. Intuitively, even the more rigid determinists mean by "nature" something more than randomly mutated genes, or natural selection for meaningless species survival, or pointless replication to no end at all. Every naturalist in this fierce war over sex is something of a teleologist despite himself. Norman Mailer is perhaps the most striking of these diffident quasi-teleogists, but they all know, their determinism notwithstanding, that their very capacity to comprehend the forces that condition them compromises their supposed servitude. They all sense that we cannot really define human nature without some reference to human ends, however dependent on human beginnings those ends may be.

It is not enough, however, for the combatants to intuit some inkling of these dialectical interconnections, for they pursue their war as if these interconnections did not exist, unaware that the interplay between the animal and the divine in human beings has a concrete impact on notions of society and culture that promises peace. The polity, from the perspective I am urging, neither limits human nature to the animal nor propels it toward the divine; rather, it provides precisely those conditions that moderate our middling humanity. Animals cannot live in polities (lion prides and wolf packs notwithstanding); divinities presumably do not need to. Civilization, with its conventions, its rituals, its symbols and customs, *is* what it means to be human. In asserting that "man is a political animal," a *zoon politikon*, Aristotle meant to suggest that it was our being-in-the-polity that gave to us our humanity. The symbolic systems of language, logic, science, and art on which society rests define our nature: not as animal, although the polity serves animal needs (the satisfaction of interests), and not as divinity, although the polity also embodies our aspirations to transcendence (religion, ethics, justice, art); but as humans who transcend animality without achieving divinity.

Despite the rather abstract character of these remarks, they have a direct bearing on the woman's question that is our real concern. For they suggest that the war for and against nature is doomed to irrelevance as long as it construes women and men as isolated creatures who, as gods or beasts, must face their destinies alone, find liberty on their own, come to terms with nature by themselves. Our human identity is given by our membership in the collective species, by our participation in the polity. The problem of liberation is thus fundamentally a social problem. Personal self-realization is always a function of collective identity, human liberation always conditioned by some social setting—the family, the clan, the voluntary association, the community of shared belief, the town, even the nation or state. The naturalist's caged animal and the liberationist's autonomous divinity are solitary creatures blessed with a self-sufficiency that makes them either more or less than human; whether fortunate or cursed, they do not resemble us. Which is why the debate as it has been carried on between the dualists has been so arid, so abstract, so removed from the everyday dilemmas that face women and men trying to live that lifetime of interdependency to which the human condition condemns us.

I do not mean to suggest there is no problem, no dilemma—only that it is an essentially social and political dilemma arising out of the conflict between needs and aspirations, between the demands we make of our institutions as heterosexual animals and those we make as conscious persons seeking equity and justice. Civilization must somehow reconcile the "natural" roles that attend sexual differentiation and the division of labor—woman-the-nester and man-the-hunter, or woman-the-reproducer and man-the-producer, for example—with the artificial personhood enjoyed by all members of just polities. Sexual differences cannot be pretended away; yet the institutions which acknowledge them must also serve human aspirations. At the level of aspirations, women and men are alike, possessing the same impulse towards transcendence, the same right to equity, the same yearning for self-realization, the same pervasively human longing for eternity that has marked civilization from its earliest beginnings. Men and women may have distinctive bodies with divergent biological capacities and emotional propensities, but they share a common human soul, a common personhood. The content mother, baby at her breast, nonetheless longs for an eternity her children cannot give her: for it is neither biological continuity nor genetic immortality she craves, but a permanent home for her soul. The pregnant wife, at the very moment her quickening womb tells her she is a sexual being in need of differential (and deferential) treatment, remains an autonomous being in need of the full rights of equity. Her vulnerability as a prospective mother is not a warrant to neglect her aspirations as a person; any more than the bent back of the field worker is a warrant to enslave his inner soul. How much frustration and bitterness women might be saved, were naturalists and their mute supporters to recognize the dialectical character of human nature.

It is, of course, simpler to annotate these dualities than to resolve them. To discover—to invent—institutions that can maintain the equal right of all to personhood while taking into account the differing needs of heterosexuality and reproduction is not an easy enterprise. The idea of sexual complementarity does not necessarily lend itself to the ideal of moral equality. Institutions arising out of natural custom and institutions derived from conscious will may precipitate radically different standards for what constitutes a human need; from convention and from artifice can come very different ideas of what an ideal institution is. Yet the quest for such institutions ought to be at the very center of the political discussion of woman's rights. It is not. Instead, the war rages on about whether we are sex-forged animals or self-forged gods, whether we are to be solitary slaves of nature or solitary automatons of free will. The only alternatives offered are to flee nature and the institutions it has stamped with its necessitarian brand to an abstract, asocial personhood conceived in solitude and enjoyed in isolation—the suburban mother who abandons her husband and abjures her maternity in an uprooting that takes her to a large, friendless city where she can pursue career ambitions and the realization of an invented, asocialized self seems to be the ideal; or to acknowledge the illusion of liberation and accept the inevitability of permanent inequality with its animal compensations—Mother Hubbard resigned to sowhood, content to know only the sociability of her squealing brood.

Certain naturalists have affected to evade the dilemma altogether by engaging in a species of hypocrisy that would be beyond comment were it not for its apparently endless popular appeal. The liberationists may be correct, the deceit goes, we probably are more than animals. *Men*, that is. Not women. In possession of whole bodies, they have no need for souls. Men, poor creatures, bereft of primary instruments of reproduction, only peripherally involved in fertilization, have what really amount to compensatory souls—"surrogate powers" in Steven

Goldberg's phrase, that fill the inner void where wombs should be. There is no natural conflict. Men are persons by default—in lieu of uteri as it were; only the unnatural resentments of women refusing to be the lucky sexual animals they "naturally" are creates a problem.

The patent wrongness of this diversionary conceit is the subject of more critical attention in Section Three. For the moment it can be accepted that both women and men behave in ways that demonstrate their common dialectical character as beings caught in the overlapping patterns of animality and divinity, equally human in their dependence on one another, equally tragic in the unfulfillable cravings of their souls. How very alike they are: men, fueled by testosterone, their penises raised as hopeful standards, are thrust by their animal natures into life—compelled to work, doomed to fight, destined to possess, unable to resist, they know not why; and women, slaves of childbirth, robbed by nature again and again of the troubled fruits of their wombs, vulnerable despite their strengths, likewise propelled down natural paths carved out for them by their own distinctive sexuality. And yet, somehow, women and men alike resist this irresistible and often comforting servitude to nature with aspirations and resolve that are no less intrinsic to the human condition—seeking liberation with souls indifferent to the constraints of sexuality, putting productivity to work to overcome the scarcity that hitherto has made productivity compulsory, transforming the natural bondage of childbirth into a rational option requiring willed justification, and always insisting, obstinately insisting in the face of blind instinct, that reasons be given for all that instinct compels.

To confound such paradoxical creatures as these with mere animals or mere divinities, to assess their dilemmas without reference to the interdependence and sociability that define the human condition, is further to enhance the confusion spread by the war between nature and liberation. Families, relationships, polities are more than integral to the problem: they define the women and men whose compound identities constitute the problem. At their best they permit the sexes to join in a mutual quest for personal freedom and human equality as they continue to serve the distinctive sexual and reproductive needs of males and females. The just polity serves not neuters but women and men, adjusting the demands of equity to meet the needs of sexual differentiation. The just marriage serves not simply women and men, but aspiring persons, accommodating sexual complementarity in a framework supportive of personal self-realization.

Not that modern nation states are just polities, or modern marriages just partnerships. On the whole, the gargantuan bureaucracies of industrial civilization are satisfied to cage the aggressive animal lurking in the shadowed past of humanity (the constitutional state) while feeding the hungry beast which, caged, can be trusted only on a full stomach (the welfare state). But this is exactly why the attention of champions of liberation ought to be directed at the rethinking and remaking of our political and social institutions rather than at the

abstract psychology of liberating women and men from
their roots in nature and society. Naturalists and liberationists share an unfortunate distaste for political argument. The former cannot see society for the animals they
think it disguises. The latter have opted for an anarchic
individualism that mistakes disintegration for liberation
a good deal of the time. Neither is sufficiently conscious
of the social requisites of freedom, neither seems to perceive how vulnerable we are when we are alone, how
necessary our mutual dependency is.

"What I discovered in the midst of my drive towards
emancipation," reports Ingrid Bengis, weary of the war
she feels she cannot avoid, "was that sex, love, hurt and
hate was the real stuff I was made of." And yet, as the
pain and passion that drive us to liberation betray our
rootedness in an animality we cannot shake off, so too the
transcendent eloquence with which we insist upon our
animal roots betrays a hint of the divine. André Malraux
thus writes bemusedly: "The mystery is not that we
should have been thrown down here at random between
the profusion of matter and that of the stars; it is that
from our very prisons we should draw from ourselves
images powerful enough to deny our nothingness."

It is a long way from Eden to Paradise, from birth to
death, from the steaming jungles to Mount Olympus.
The journey cannot be made alone. Although the animals from whom we come and the gods to whom we are
drawn may live in solitude, our human pilgrimage is
held together by bonds of interdependence no woman or
man dare break. Mutuality is the strength of the species.

We are too trapped to be wholly free, yet free enough to rattle our chains with a noise the gods can hear.

These remarks constitute a preliminary sketch of the perspective from which the concrete tasks of this book are undertaken. But abstractions cannot serve either nature or liberation. The real issue of women's freedom in contemporary Western society begs for solutions no generalities can bring. The point then must be to justify the possibility of an alternative to war through a careful inquiry into the positions taken by the radical feminists —the most thorough and serious of the liberationists engaged in the war against nature; and through an equally exacting look at the counteroffensive against liberation being waged by the adversaries of radical feminism.

With the war better understood, the terms of peace suggested here but spelled out in terms of the particular problems of modern women can be introduced, and the programmatic implications of such a peace raised. The goal is to put an end to the war and thereby liberate feminism from its abstractness, its anomie, its apoliticality, its uprootedness. A feminism thus liberated will no longer have to require enmity to men and alienation from self as the price of emancipation; instead, it will promise to both women and men the only kind of freedom the human condition permits: self-realization in the distinctively human environment of loving families and the just polity.

2

The War on Nature, or Misunderstanding Liberation

"BEING A WOMAN," said Joseph Conrad, "must be a terribly difficult trade, since it consists principally of dealings with men." And to men, women have forever been a mystery—less a separate gender than an alien species to be prudently admired or nervously ridiculed, but almost never understood. Eternally misperceived, women have been systematically disadvantaged: undereducated or overprotected, denied employment or unequally remunerated, excluded from the professions then excoriated as inept, driven to the limits of reason then indicted as hysterical. Women have been used as property, abused as servants, neglected as things, patronized as children, idealized as fictions and enshrined as myths. When they have not been belittled by vilification, they have been maligned by idolatry.

No wonder then that among thoughtful women the cry, "Let my people go!" is uttered with increasing frequency and escalating bitterness. No wonder that impa-

tient feminists are ready to discard men, give up children, reject if necessary their own reproductive identities to gain a foundation for their liberty. There is hardly
a complaint in the too-ancient litany of woman's grievances that is not founded on some real injury, some per-
sistent abuse, some irrefutable indignity. Hardly a
woman's aspiration has not at some time been ob-
structed, deformed or mocked. And always in the name
of sexuality, of biology, of nature.

Understandably enough, the movement that has
arisen in response to these grievances has declared war
on nature. Unhappily, this means that it has joined
forces with many elements in the society it challenges,
that it has been infected with the contradictions that
created the iniquitous conditions it deplores. The rebels
find themselves re-enslaved by the tools that sever their
chains, and only irony is well served. This seems inevitable in an all-out war against nature in a culture whose
dominant institutions are themselves hostile to nature—
if in the name of efficiency rather than liberty, control
rather than liberation. Despite its benevolent radicalism,
feminism thus seems weighed down with the baggage of
our times: with the misconceptions of liberalism, the
parochialisms of media fashion, the anachronisms of last
century's Marxism, the technologism of voguish science,
the narcissism of a middle class that complacently reads
the world as an extension of itself. It is rather more
symptomatic of than remedial to the national uprootedness that has long infected this frontier land. Foundering
under the weight of all this ideological baggage, the liberationist movement sometimes seems reduced to foist-

ing abstractions on an uncertain constituency whose real grievances are distorted to conform to the shape of an inchoate but defiant utopia. As such, it does not always serve the meaningful amelioration of woman's condition as well as it might, while it inadvertantly risks enhancing the potency of the most dangerous establishmentarian biases: uniformity, technocracy, irresponsibility, hedonism, narcissism, and mindless innovation for its own pointless sake—biases which, not so incidentally, share a common contempt for both nature and the human polity.

Some care needs to be exercised in asserting that there is a "woman's movement" possessing a singular, identifiable ideology. Unlimited caution is called for in trying to characterize the views of women whose positions range from the housewife hoping for an afternoon, a checkbook or a room of her own, to the technocratic Amazon aspiring to the (if necessary violent) annihilation of sexual differentiation and the (if necessary permanent) extirpation of men. Nevertheless, if there is to be rational discourse at all, general characterizations must be hazarded; and if that discourse is not to bog down in endless syntactical involutions whose caveats and modifiers permit no single sentence ever to be terminated, a certain license must be granted for generalization. Thus, while acknowledging the rich variety of views among feminists and apologizing for the neglect any one generalization may evince for particular liberationist standpoints, I intend nevertheless to proceed on the assumption that a few rather general premises are held in common by most feminists and that together these premises do suggest a generally coherent position. Specifically, liberationists seem to have claimed in the past ten years that

- women are oppressed, both by nature and by the appeal to nature;
- men and marriage are natural obstacles to women's human fulfillment as persons;
- monogamous marriage and the nuclear family are crucial instruments in capitalism's system of natural exploitation;
- romantic love is the ideology of naturalist sexism;

and finally, most significantly, that

- femininity and natural sexual differentiation are inimical to and ultimately incompatible with human equality and liberated personhood;

this final claim being inseperable from the liberationist war on nature.

While these interdependent claims are accepted to a greater or lesser degree by individual feminists, and while particular ones may reject one or another of them outright, I intend to treat them *tout court* under the general heading feminism. I want to look at the first four claims at once, in some detail. The final proposition, which is at the core of the liberationist position, demands independent treatment after both the liberationist and naturalist positions have been evaluated.

I.

At the very center of the feminist ideology is the conviction that women are by nature the "most oppressed of all people" (Juliet Mitchell), that sexist oppression is even "more endemic to our society than racism" (Kate Millet), that sexism represents the "oldest, most rigid class/caste system in existence" (Shulamith Firestone). These claims echo the urgency of traditional feminism in their impassioned rhetoric. The Woman's Rights Convention at Seneca Falls in 1848 proclaimed,

> "The history of mankind is a history of repeated injuries and usurpations on the part of man toward woman, having as its direct object the establishment of tyranny over her."

From then until now, the relative isolation of women in otherwise egalitarian societies from power and status has probably necessitated an inflamed rhetoric. To the deaf the most blood-curdling screams may be heard as whispers: who then can blame the shouters? But such rhetoric is more useful in war than discourse; today, more often than not, it seems to reflect the unhappy linguistic inflation that has become almost mandatory for dissenters wishing to attract the attention of a jaundiced mass media, and hoping to gain a tactical advantage over competing "oppressed" groups. The language of rebellion has already been transmogrified and appropriated by consumer capitalism: compact cars are "rebels," cream

depilatories are radical innovations, vaginal deodorants
are unprecedented discoveries in a revolutionary technology and "Freedom is just another word for Datsun."
What is left for authentic radicals? Phrase-starved dissi-
dents are forced to verbal escalation if their war is to be
publicized: discrimination becomes tyranny, abuse
becomes slavery, role differentiation becomes servitude
and inequality becomes oppression.

Yet the rhetoric of war aside, pertinent historical and
contemporary standards would seem to argue that
women in Western industrial societies are not *oppressed*;
and that those who speak with the most vigor about
oppression (white, middle-class, urban/suburban professional women)—as is typical in most so-called revolutions of rising expectations—are perhaps least oppressed
of all. Abused, mistreated, discriminated against, patronized, put down, misused, conned, neglected, wronged,
deceived and more—but not oppressed. Hurt, restless,
bitter, discontent, bored, frustrated, impatient and an-
gry—but not enslaved. By the same token, men may be
stupid, abusive, self-indulgent, childish, short-sighted,
callous, blind, insensitive and oafish—but they are not
oppressors.

These are, at the level of rhetoric, petty distinctions,
and an abused woman may want to reply, "Call my
condition what you please: you will not improve it by
giving it a sweeter name." But even at the level of rhetoric, the term oppression is no mere label. It is a crucial
legitimizing ticket in those ignominious sweepstakes
through which radical movements have been seduced
into undoing themselves by feeling obliged to outdo oth-

ers. When Yoko Ono says "woman is the nigger of the world," she indulges in a tragic kind of lexicographical slumming that aspires to capture the righteous mana of other persons' suffering with the magic of words. Like so many white, middle-class students of the 1960s, feminists have been driven into insisting not only that they are oppressed, but that they are *more* oppressed than blacks, *more* oppressed than any toiling proletariat, that they are the *most* oppressed of all peoples. This can cause discord where there ought to be mutual support. Linda J. M. La Rue, a young black woman writing in *Trans-Action* in 1970, evinced considerable anger in contemplating her white sister's empathetic espousal of "niggerdom":

> Let it be stated unequivocally that the American white woman has had a better opportunity to live a free and fulfilling life, both mentally and physically, than any other group in the United States, excluding her white husband. Thus any attempt to analogize black oppression with the plight of the American white woman has all the validity of comparing the neck of a hanging man with the rope-burned hands of an amateur mountain climber.

If—she seems to say—if the white, middle-class housewife, for all her very real frustrations, is to be called oppressed, then what are we to call the homeless, impoverished, addicted, black school dropout? Or the victim of Buchenwald? If, as Kate Millet has it, we are to understand "coitus as killing," then what is homicidal rape? What is murder? Rhetorical metaphors are perhaps unavoidable in a literary war, but this set of usages brings too readily to mind such Department of Defense neologisms as "overkill" and "mega-deaths."

It remains vital, in a responsible reform movement, to distinguish, for example, the professional woman who makes only $12,000 per annum instead of the $20,000 given her male counterpart *because she is a woman*, from the Appalachian hillswoman who is uneducated and unemployable at any price *because she is poor*; or to distinguish the New Jersey coed ballplayer who is excluded from the Little League because she is "only a girl" from the Vietnamese coed who is raped, eviscerated and murdered because she is "only a gook." Suffering is not necessarily a fixed and universal experience that can be measured by a single rod: it is related to situations, needs and aspirations. But there must be some historical and political parameters for use of the term so that political priorities can be established and different forms and degrees of suffering can be given the most appropriate kinds of attention. A broken bone is serious, but a massive coronary requires prior attention, however insistently the patient with the fracture may cry, "I am dying!" Nora's plight in Ibsen's *A Doll's House* is troubling, but it is not Anne Frank's plight at Buchenwald: one is harrassed, the other imprisoned, one awakening to the possibilities of her potential freedom, the other deprived of her actual freedom, one at war with inner ambivalence and cultural conditioning, the other at war with external enemies and physical persecution. Neither woman is to be denied, but their situations are very different. When Nora finally decides her husband and her family stand in the way of her self-realization, no bars on the window or locks on the door impede her exit to "freedom." Her husband's confused self-pity and pleading tears are the only instruments raised against her and they are no match at all for her will. What prisoner of the Warsaw ghetto or of the state penitentiary can walk to freedom by a mere act of self-recognition? What victim of racism or economic oppression can simply decide to be free?

The grievances of women are serious and compelling enough without confounding them with oppression. Indeed, tactically considered, nothing is more likely to invite belittlement than the comparative perspective evoked by terms like oppression and tyranny. The cry, "We have been abused" from the abused provokes attention and compels change, but the assertion, "We are victims of total oppression" from the abused is all too easily dismissed, along with the just complaints it is meant to dramatize. It is not a matter of crying wolf, but far more dangerous, of crying "earthquake!" when wolves are truly on the prowl. Nor is this merely a tactical consideration. The appeal to a radical and total oppression creates an invidiously polarized climate where only radical and total solutions seem possible, where the destruction of sexism becomes synonymous with the annihilation of sexuality, where the creative tension between nature and freedom gives way to uncompromising war against nature.

The war on nature in turn entails that oppression be regarded as endemic to the very nature of femininity, to the natural relations of the sexes as conditioned by biology. It is not the abuse of sexuality but sexuality—or more properly, heterosexuality—itself that is to be in-dicted. It is a strange way to speak, but feminists often seem obliged to say that women are oppressed by their very own nature—their cursed menses, their hormonal passivity, their maternal vulnerability, their inter-dependency with men. Yet it seems certain to me that the abuse of women is something done *to* not *by* their natures—is an attribute of their relationship to men, not intrinsic to it.

This is a critical distinction, for oppression is better understood as a particular kind of relationship than as a feature of relationships in general: namely, a relation-ship which is intrinsically and consciously exploitative. To speak of oppression is to speak of those instances of overt human usury where one class of beings literally (not figuratively or metaphorically) and deliberately (not accidentally or incidentally) crushes and enslaves an-other, coercing them into a condition of abject, involun-tary servitude. What is significant about oppression is that it *constitutes* the relationship between oppressed and oppressor. Without it there would be no relationship at all. Capitalists and workers are, in the Marxist frame-work, defined in their relations by exploitation. It is the oppressive connection that differentiates them. Like-wise, whites and blacks in pre-Civil War America (and probably in the post bellum epoch as well) were defined in their roles of master and slave by oppression. What-ever else might have happened between them as people, the only formal relationship that bound them together was oppression.

But the relationship between women and men has

never been intrinsically exploitative or oppressive, the assault on naturalism notwithstanding. Its basis has been, at the level of nature, hormonal differentiation, sexual magnetism and the requisites of heterosexual reproduction; and at the level of culture, childrearing, companionship, complementarity and love. The role *Woman*, however often it has been abused, is not defined by abuse. Masters quite literally invent slaves, in order to invent themselves, just as capitalists dialectically invent the proletariat. But it can hardly be said that men invent women, and no amount of controversy about cultural conditioning or the manipulative stereotypes of the male literary imagination can change this paramount fact. As ever before, women still give birth to men, and though men have contrived to return the favor—in Genesis for example—heterosexuality is a biological reality for which they cannot claim credit.

The natural fact of heterosexuality and the complementarity it suggests points to another distinctive feature of female-male relations as against other varieties of human interaction. While different cultural, racial or national groups have evolved independently and then encountered one another as monolithic wholes, under conditions of competition or enmity where differences could be made the basis of domestication or subjugation of one by the other, women and men have cohabited the world together from its prehistorical beginnings. They are not two alien races thrown together by geopolitical accident, but two versions of humanity who have shared a common destiny, two individually insufficient parts of a species made whole only by each other. Like most other animals, human beings come in pairs. Whatever men have done to women, or women to men, it cannot be fruitfully compared to the oppressive subjugation of the "barbarians" (whether Persian, Mongolian or African) by their crusading enemies (whether Greek, Chinese or European).

If women and men are construed as natural aliens whose differences correspond to that infernal set of artificial distinctions by which our species has justified its great bigotries and lesser envies, there is little doubt that the war of all against all will finally destroy us. In our heterosexuality lies the last hope for mutualism: when the family is perceived as but one more disguise for interest assertion and domination, when the polity is defamilialized and the family politicized, the disintegration of society cannot be very far off. This is why it is so important that those concerned with treating the inequities of the present condition be certain of what the problem is, prudent in their choice of key terms. Oppression will do, as rhetoric, to scare the hell out of those sniggering bigots who cannot quite decide whether to jeer or leer at aspirations that—they pretend—go no further than the shedding of bras. It will not do as discourse, as argument, as an analysis of what is wrong and what is to be done. For it suggests solutions that are little better than the problems. If we insist that relations between the sexes are primarily exploitative (Kate Millet's perception of sexual relations as sexual politics), then the only logical remedy is the elimination of sexual differentiation— the eradication of sexuality itself (although Millet and others do not always pursue logic to its conclusion). This

in turn requires excesses that, even as rhetoric, are out-
landish. It can be achieved only by eliminating men (or,
presumably, women); or by negating all salient differences between the sexes in pursuit of androgyny (the
clitoris as penis, the dildo as equalizer, the orgasm as
common denominator); or by circumventing human
physiology in favor of technological surrogates (artificial
insemination, cloning, extra-uteral gestation).

Probably only a few self-consciously pioneering radicals in the woman's movement take these measures seriously, but they reflect a thrust that can affect even the
most moderate programs for change. War permits no
neutrals. Once nature is regarded as the foe, moderation
can look treasonous. Heterosexual women in groups
dominated by lesbians know how easy it is to feel genuinely guilty about trafficking in heterosexual feelings or
relating affirmatively to men, and in large cities the demand for equal pay may be put forward apologetically
by women who fear they will appear reactionary for
asking so little.

If, however, we begin with the premise that sexual
relations between women and men, however perverted
by abuse or corrupted by socioeconomic exploitation
they may be in a particular culture, are essentially
healthy and desirable, then the avenue to emancipation
is less tortuous. To immunize marital and familial relations against corruption is an enterprise different in degree and kind from the treatment required for structural
or congenital corruption. If marriage is a cancer, it must
be destroyed; if it has cancer it can be saved, providing
the treatment distinguishes the natural organ from the

invading infection. The task is restorative rather than revolutionary, reconstructive not eradicative. Nature can be an ally in the struggle to contain corruption, and a feminism that hopes to be liberating need no longer proceed as if artifice were its only ally.

The feminist position may not, however, always seem susceptible to this kind of criticism; for the argument that women are oppressed has frequently been inverted, so that it takes the more aggressive form "men and marriage are natural obstacles to women's self-fulfillment as persons." This provocative claim needs to be considered on another level.

II.

Where there are oppressed, there must be oppressors: enter Men. "Women," Germaine Greer writes, "have very little idea of how much men hate them." The more tolerant feminists will concede that the role men have played has to some degree been involuntary, more the product of nature than of malevolence. Greer, for example, allows that "men do not themselves know the depth of their hatred." To others, the role is perceived as knowingly chauvinistic, explicitly coercive, intentionally oppressive. As before, we can attribute some of this to rhetorical escalation. Elaine Morgan is much more realistic when she writes, in *The Descent of Women*:

> You may raise the alarm and beat the drum, but when you point your finger at [men] the enemy, most [women] will say: "No, no, those aren't leopards. That's the postman,

and that one is my son, and the one with the nice blue eyes is the one who was so kind to us last winter when there was all that snow." And they will be right.

Yet a great deal of very real resentment exists, for there is hardly a woman living who cannot recall being abused, hurt, and otherwise—to use an expression which makes its own case—manhandled by the sex to which they are told to look for comfort and protection. At the same time, women, like men, have experienced considerable grief not occasioned by their relations with the other sex which nevertheless somehow gets blamed on partners. As a consequence, real threats to the opportunities and status of women are lost sight of in a general indictment that is too sweeping ever to lead to any concrete convictions.

Many of the deprivations suffered by women are the result of bad marriages or abusive men, but these are too often confounded with the deprivations that grow out of the insufficiency of being, the elusiveness of happiness, the transience of meaning in an era that has abdicated faith, declared war on nature, severed its links with the past and left only the arrogance of a soulless technology between itself and an inchoate, hostile universe. Some feminists seem to expect of life not merely opportunity but fulfillment, not a lonely search for relative meaning but the final discovery of absolute truth, not a license for living but a guaranteed warrant for happiness. And then, when life is not forthcoming, a conspirator is conjured up to explain the failure of expectations. Certain feminists attribute to the perversity of men, frustrations

endemic to their humanity. "It is so much easier," Ingrid
Bengis writes in *Combat in the Erogenous Zone*, "to say love
is bullshit than to get over a love affair, so much easier
to speak of oppression than to confess to private pain, so
much easier in the long run to hate men than to love
them." Unhappily, such candor comes more easily to
sensitive writers like Bengis and Erica Jong than to par-
tisans in the war on nature.

Marriage too suffers as a scapegoat in the campaign to
identify the sources of oppression; Kathrin Perutz's book
needs only its title to reveal its intent—*Marriage Is Hell*.
Marital relations, the indictment reads, are usually
possessive, abusive and inimical to growth. Probably
true. But only because human relations are usually
possessive, abusive and inimical to growth. And this
only because humankind appears, in its animal nature,
all too predisposed to possessiveness (because we are insufficient?), abusiveness (because we fear our dependency?), and stagnation (because growth is so painful?).
Doctor Johnson observed, "Marriage is not commonly
unhappy otherwise than as life is unhappy." Separating
out what is life and what is marriage has been difficult
for feminists. Are things any different among the unmarried? Or is the problem really human relations? College
roommates fight, brothers and sisters display envy, enmity and selfishness, friends can become morosely dependent, business partners have been known to liquidate
one another along with their partnerships, lesbians can
be as spiteful as spouses, and communards—the new
utopians of those who do not live in communes—live
under conditions that can be "a microcosm of every form

of international terror and paranoia" (Elia Katz, in *Armed Love*). Why pin the rap for the whole human race on marriage?

Kate Millet was recently sued by three of her colleagues in the making of the film *Three Lives*. Following the trial, one of the plaintiffs (Leonore Bode) supposedly accused Millet of being "divisive, manipulative. . . as much a male chauvinist as any man." Which is to say, women too are human, possessed of human frailties even as they fight for liberation. Bengis again seizes on realities with an awesome veracity. "What are we going to do," she asks, "if it turns out that women are just as fucked up as men?" If liberation depends on proving that men are a great deal more fucked up than women, liberation will presumably have to be abandoned. But that is exactly why casting men as villains is so fruitless an exercise. The sorts of villainy associated with men and marriage are universal and suggest there is no hope for change at all; what we need to know, if we are to improve our relations, is what is wrong with marriage—specifically, concretely, uniquely—not what is wrong with the species.

Yet marriage, some may want to reply, *is* uniquely and concretely and specifically stultifying. It compels partners into a lifelong relationship that moves ineluctably from spontaneity and freshness to regularity and boredom; and thence, as medicine extends already hapless lives into the seventies and eighties, to an emotional deadening from which there can be no recovery. This too is true. But again, only because many men and women, married and single, ossify at the first approach of middle age, petrify with the onset of their forties, and freeze over at fifty with a glacial certainty that is melted only by the rebirth called senility—which, however, is itself but a prelude to death.

Yes, marriage is boring. Because life is boring, all that is customary is boring; we are at one level boring to ourselves when we come to know ourselves well—that is one of the unhappy costs of emotional maturity. Marriage is boring, bachelorhood is boring, divorce is boring, spinsterhood is boring—to the degree we cannot discover inner resources and creative aims that do not depend on novelty for freshness, on adventure for spiritedness, on self-alienation for discovery. Françoise Sagan (again it is the writer who sees clearly) permits a character in her recent novel *Scars On The Soul* to say:

> The truth is that the married couple, or the individual, or the mass of people are completely deadened by a way of life that is designed to deaden them. . . and it follows from this of course. . . that the inequality of the sexes is blamed for the mutual exhaustion of a married couple.

Ultimately marriage, even in its rigid, monogamous form, only reflects the capacities and inadequacies of its partners: it does not destroy women and men, women and men destroy it.

The feminists then have misconceived the character of marriage because they have not always been completely honest with themselves about the character of life. Even at its emancipated best in loving marriages and well-ordered polities, life takes the form of necessary, ineluctable tensions, of poignant, irresoluble dilemmas that confront women and men with the painful hiatus between aspiration and achievement and mock them with the chasm between desire and fulfillment. Between the infant's fantasy of a world which is but an extension of itself and the mature being's comprehension of its own insignificance in an indifferent cosmos lies a reality into whose subtleties too many feminists have been unable or unwilling to enter. Rhetorical necessity and the spirited elan of combat have desensitized them to the fact that alienation is something more than a female disorder occassioned by the malice of men, that insufficiency and a sense of apartness have been our species' fate since Eden —or since that Paleolithic separation from the animal kingdom to which Eden pays somber tribute.

Dependency is the universal condition of the race, not a proprietary disease of married women. Moreover, dependency produces a natural scarcity of the inner life, less economic than existential, that puts the costs of solitary self-realization very high. There has always been a price on living among our fellow creatures in ways that we can understand as human—a price demanded by the delicate ecology of human relations that permits radical independence only at the cost of estrangement and solitude, that requires of love vulnerability, that makes each choice interdependent with each other choice and makes every consequence a foil to every other consequence.

Ask Isadora Wing. Isadora Wing plays a sort of Henrietta Miller in Erica Jong's *Fear Of Flying*. One of those incorrigibles who finds the truth too comic to bother with self-deception and is better at recognizing painful decisions than making them. Isadora Wing has plenty of hubris but no illusions:

> I had never been able to make peace between the two halves of myself. All I had managed to do was suppress one half (for awhile) at the expense of the other. I had never been happy with the bourgeois virtues of marriage, stability, and work above pleasure. I was too curious and adventurous not to chafe under those restrictions. But I also suffered from night terrors and attacks of panic at being alone. So I always wound up living with somebody or being married. . . there just didn't seem any way to get the best of both exuberance and stability in your life.

Or love and self-reliance; or comfortable familiarity and vertiginous novelty. Isadora Wing knows.

What she knows is a better starting point for understanding the realities that condition our present situation and must inform the direction of potential reforms than the rhetoric of an abstract war on nature. There are multiple evils that have been grafted onto the natural plight of the race that can and ought to be cut away. Naturalists who use the human plight as a metaphysical redoubt for complacency and inaction in facing the particular plight of women and men now are merely masking prejudices in ethological speculation. But to confound the remediable abuses of woman's condition with the irremediable abuses of the human condition only diverts the search for improved human relations to a quest for meta-human deliverance.

The inalterable dilemmas of our existential condition

are futilely dramatized while the alterable corruptions with which we have managed to embellish that already infelicitous condition spread unchecked and unnoticed. For example, while certain science-crazed feminists seek technological surrogates for maternity, mothers look for more personal, sensitized forms of childbirth. While the vanguard propounds manless communes for child-rearing, rank and file wives wonder how to involve their husbands more meaningfully in the rearing of their children. Movement rhetoric calls for the liberation of children, while worried parents wonder where their teenagers are at three o'clock in the morning, and whether Peter's "wrestling bruises" are not really track marks like the ones in the movie shown at the PTA. And while ideology demands that marriage be condemned, it continues to dominate society—frightening divorce rates having no effect at all on soaring marriage rates—confirming again that the issue we face is not how to abolish the institution but how to make it more workable, more loving, more nourishing, and more permanent.

It is both misleading and unjust to suggest, however, that feminist vision suffers from unique ideological cataracts. There is no middle-class political reform movement in America today that is not to some degree afflicted by an intolerance for complexity and subtlety, a self-indulgent and finally self-defeating narcissism, an existential anxiety that issues as much from enervating leisure as from injustice. The warriors are, after all, no less conditioned by the society they assail than the establishmentarians who glower from its defensive parapets.

Intolerance for ambiguity can be found in almost every corner of our labile society. It is a society which, as its dilemmas and frustrations multiply, looks more and more to simplistic cure-alls: to demagogic politics, to efficient technologism, to the illusory dogmas of a "science of human behavior." A perversely common thread runs through the lowbrow predilection for unambivalent political solutions and the highbrow predilection for efficacious technological solutions, a thread that knits chauvinist nationalism and religious fundamentalism together with vulgar behavioralism and the worship of science into a single appalling pattern. Each reflects a sense of individual, inner impotence, each looks to totalistic, external solutions for intractable problems, each seeks simplified, reductionist explanations for overwhelmingly complex realities—law and order for society, orderly laws for human behavior, everything neat, tidy and in place.

The media fairly ooze with panaceas. Problems are not confronted, they are skirted with groundless optimism, silver-lined with banalities. Is your marriage of half a lifetime breaking up? Not a problem but an opportunity: read *Creative Divorce*. Do you think prostitution degrades women? Read *The Happy Hooker*. Runaway inflation, a world energy crisis and the breakdown of the international monetary structure need not trouble those who read *How To Profit From A Monetary Crisis*; and for the less ambitious with less ambitious ailments, there is *How I Turn Ordinary Complaints into Thousands of Dollars*. Panaceas are everywhere. Look at our political mentors, our culture heroes, our book awards, our bestseller lists, our magazine cover stories over the last decade—panaceas, panaceas, panaceas: a respite from choas through law, order and the Bomb (Goldwater, Wallace et al.); interpersonal harmony through behavior modification and environmental conditioning (B.F.Skinner); rebirth of the cities through the expansion of bureacracy ("The Great Society"); human relatedness through meaningless touching (Desmond Morris) or parlor games (Eric Berne) or pop psychology *(I'm O.K.–You're O.K.)*; world community through the universal philistinism of television (Marshall McLuhan); love through terminal sentimentality (Erich Segal) or through seagulls (Jonathan Livingston); rebellion through buffoonery (Abbie Hoffman or S.C.U.M.); revolution through peanut-butter (Charles Reich); self-realization through orgasm through technique (Masters and Johnson and the ubiquitous *Joy of Sex)*; ecology through consumerism *(The Last Whole Earth Catalog,* which turned out to be only the first); Nirvana through LSD (Timothy Leary); wisdom through astrodomed gurus (Maharaj Ji) and rabbits *(Watership Down)*; and peace through war, truth through lies, honor through deceit and winning through just abou anything it takes (Richard Nixon—though it did not save him in the end). The easier, the better. The sooner, the better. The simpler, the better. The more painless, the better.

In the face of this desperate plasticity, this society-wide quest for a cultural anesthetic, only a partisan misogynist could isolate feminism's penchant for unambiguous answers and total solutions. When Jill Johnston intimates in the *Village Voice* that lesbian motherhood may somehow be an improvement on heterosexual parenthood, when Shulamith Firestone suggests that since "the material basis for sexual division is in the reproductive system, the revolutionary means to its annihilation will be man's scientific ability to transcend it," when digital-clitoral stimulation is thought of as an adequate alternative to sexual intercourse and liberation from sexism can no longer be distinguished from the obliteration of sexuality, feminism is merely joining the ongoing American revolution—with its safe, breezy rhetoric, its box-office sensationalism, its unfortunate detachment from the difficult realities of both injustice and reform. In a way it is not even fair to expect that feminism should be any different. Except that its battle is being waged on behalf of liberation, against the bonfires consuming our culture. Burning up the fire truck may call attention to the perils of fire but it is not likely to extinguish the larger conflagration.

Unhappily, feminism has also been much too vulnerable to the willful narcissism that has left so many Americans in permanent adolescence. In the society at large, pervasive consumerism and the acquisitive mentality it nourishes have encouraged the survival of the pubescent ego far beyond its normal life span. The commercial deification of youth and the contempt for age that is its corrolary act to legitimate this truncation of the maturation process. Consequently, young adults, especially those most sensitized to the hypocrisies of adult society, have insisted on remaining children. Student rebels demand radical change, but eschew any permanent responsibility; young communards seek human contact and the personalization of social relations, but seem unprepared for commitment and incapable of sustaining intimacy. Yet who can blame them for resisting adulthood when to be adult means to lie persuasively, kill honorably, toil mindlessly and self-destruct willingly? When responsibility means justifying genocide, realism means selling out to money, and loyalty, power and commitment mean dismembering the constitution to patch up the Presidency?

Liberationists in the woman's movement, in many cases troubled by the same sensitivity, the same outraged idealism, have been caught up in this same self-indulgence. For all the rhetoric, they shrink back, prudently we might say, from the overwhelming power of the status quo, and develop strategies geared to a modest selfishness that is at least feasible. Ellen Peck's *The Baby Trap* typifies this unfortunate narcissism. "The birth of children," she complains, "too often means the dissolution of romance, the loss of freedom, the abandonment of ideals to economics." Or there is Jill Johnston, more candid than she is prudent, revealing "I had to let my children go to become myself." Go where? "Children's liberation" becomes an ambivalent slogan when children bear children. It is hard not to believe that it is the "parents'" lingering childhood that is at stake. Liberate the children ends up meaning abandon the children so the parents can go free. "Certainly none of us were told," Johnston continues, "what a drastic drag it was to become a mother. I mean motherhood was a soft fuzzy tinted photo." What a drastic drag, that is to say, to have to grow up, to have to defer to the needs of younger, more vulnerable beings who rudely shout, "You are grown, now me!" Although she feels forced to become a "psuedo-mother," she persists in viewing herself as a "perennial daughter." Appropriately enough, our society is perfectly satisfied with this arrangement: permanent sons and perennial daughters are after all splendidly permanent consumers and perennial subjects. Childless unmarrieds spend much more on conspicuous consumption than burdened marrieds putting all they have into insurance policies and savings accounts and college trusts.

The establishmentarian success a few years ago of Charles Reich's *The Greening of America* should astonish no one. As a passive utopia for perennial children where hip living styles were to vanquish conflict and suffering, it was a nearly perfect "revolutionary" substitute in a reactionary, capitalist society: it promised to sell goods, keeping capitalism in business, it idealized apoliticality, leaving the politicians to govern as they chose, it celebrated childish innocence, depriving the young of the maturity they had to have to bring about change, it enjoined impotence, guaranteeing power to the most venal and unscrupulous. Perennial childhood is finally no solution at all to the problem of adult identity. It evades corruption, to be sure, but at the price of foregoing responsibility and the possibilities of change.

Many women, not necessarily involved in the movement, have been rightly concerned with the infantilism of husbands who use marriage to fulfill unrealizable childhood fantasies, who make of their wives surrogate mothers. But is the radical answer to the immaturity of men to be the immaturity of women? Is the self-indulgent male ego to be checked by unbridling the female ego? Are we really to be condemned to the comfortless choice between the guilt-inspired, over-protective, interfering, vicariously manipulative parents of the last generation and the self-centered, irresponsible, rationalizing non-parents of the next, as envisioned by those seeking liberation? To the choice between smothering our children and abandoning them? Is the final equality of the sexes to be the equity of mutual infantilism? Does the war on nature require that we deny maternity, sterilize fecundity, and subject the accidents who are somehow born to Spartan exposure?

Children are the future of our species. In bearing them we confirm our belief in ourselves, while acknowledging the inevitability of individual death. Personal liberation exacts many costs and demands damaging sacrifices. But it does not and cannot call on us to terminate the species. The specific indifference to children of some feminists bears an unpleasant resemblance to society's general indifference to the future: "liberation now, and to hell with the kids!" sounds very much like "energy now, and to hell with the kids!" It may well be that traditional Protestant cultures in Europe spent too much time thinking about the future and too little giving meaning to the present. That is not our problem. In an America where planning is still "communistic" and worrying about tomorrow is "up tight," capitalists and consumers, old and young alike, are conspiring to relegate the future to an

oblivion where the past has long lain rotting. Liberationists cannot afford to take part in this conspiracy; feminists need to be rescued from it.

It is difficult, however, for if narcissism has nourished
anxieties about the ambiguous rewards of maturation
and responsibility and dulled our sense of continuity
between present and future, leisure has exacerbated the
problem unmercifully. At no time in history have so
many people in a society enjoyed so much abundance—
sufficient abundance to transform leisure from an unattainable luxury into an unavoidable burden. The world
still staggers under the yoke of economic scarcity, our
own society flourishes only by maintaining structural
poverty, a growing coterie of New Malthusians
prophesy an ecological Armageddon of which the world
energy crisis is only a foretaste; yet for all of this, the
contemporary middle class in America is for the first
time in history experiencing on behalf of the human race
some of the costs of winning the struggle with nature for
survival: endless days no amount of play can shorten,
interminable weeks with less and less work to fill them,
yawning months whose emptiness only underscores the
meaninglessness of the "good life" once the struggle to
secure it has been won.

Women—more particularly educated, middle-class,
suburban women—find themselves at the very front of
this historical tide, drowning in leisure. While their husbands absorb themselves in work, competition, fiscal responsibilities and hobbies, in trivia made significant by
desperation, women sit restlessly at home among the
gadgets that have stolen from them what little meaning

was to be found in homemaking, burdened with the existential dilemmas of the whole race: who, why, what for, am I? No, motherhood is no answer: to bear and raise two children takes only four or five intense years, another ten part-time years—there are thirty or forty more after that. Being a good wife? In a society where home and office roles are so fragmented and women socialized for independence, it is not enough—even if it were desirable which, for most women, it is not. For a long time, the only available answers were self-destructive: alcohol, adultery, divorce, daytime television and suicide. Some estimates guess that up to forty percent of attempted suicides are by housewives. Liberationists, outraged by these casualty rates, have moved in another direction—work, flight into the labor market. If this is fully understandable in a society that measures status by employment and power by income, it is also untoward in several important ways.

It has, to begin with, social costs that may be worth paying but are too often simply unconsidered. When large numbers of relatively well-educated women enter a rigid labor market in which large numbers of relatively unskilled workers are already unemployed, their employment will probably spell joblessness for many at the bottom. Nonwhite young men between sixteen and thirty, who already comprise a large proportion of the unemployed, will find it tougher than ever to get a job. At this point the need to set priorities based on some objective measure of real suffering, oppression and injustice becomes paramount, and the real costs of the feminist insistence on the term oppression become visible.

Sexism exists with and not in place of racism and economic exploitation: liberationists cannot expect the poor
to look appreciatively on what appears to be a middle-
class campaign to wrest still more jobs away from them.

The second point that needs to be made about work is
a qualification of the first. Work clearly means something very different to women in search of an escape
from leisure than it has to most of the human race for
most of history. For a few lucky men, for far fewer
women, work has occasionally been a source of meaning
and creativity. But for most of the race it remains even
now forced drudgery in front of ploughs, machines,
words or numbers—pushing products, pushing
switches, pushing papers to eke out the wherewithal of
material existence. Perhaps because well-educated middle-class women are often married to professional men
who can claim to derive a certain pleasure from jobs that
are not wholly mindless, they seem sometimes to treat
work as if it held the secret to meaning, as if it were a
coveted Hobby of the Elect greedily monopolized by the
oppressors. But oppressors are people who live off other
men's labor, not people who insist on doing all the work
themselves.

Think of the proletarian caricature of the capitalist as
a lazy, parasitic, do-nothing who sits at home enjoying an
income distilled from the blood of his workers. Among
many poorer Americans, liberation means the freedom
of a mother finally to quit her job—to live the life of a
capitalist stay-at-home as it were. Of course work for her
has meant scrubbing floors or scouring toilets or sewing
endless buttons on discount smocks, and has more to do

with self-preservation than self-realization. Even the most debasing sort of menial labor can, it is true, be perceived as an escape from the pointed dilemmas of leisure—providing it is not compulsory. To be able to work and to have to work are two very different matters. I suspect, however, that few liberationist women are to be found working as menials and unskilled laborers simply in order to occupy their time and identify with the power structure. For status and power are not conferred by work per se, but by certain kinds of work generally reserved to the middle and upper class. There is little status in washing dishes, even in the kitchen of the Four Seasons. And the clout of a dishwasher's paycheck on his family or in the economy generally can hardly rival that of a welfare check. In the end, however hard we concentrate on sexism, the economics of class, race and power creep back into the picture. As Studs Terkel shows in *Working*, most workers find jobs dull, oppressive, frustrating and alienating—very much what women find housewifery.

We may, of course—and this is the third and perhaps most disturbing irony of the liberationist attitude to work—decide as a race that we are better off under the tyranny of economic necessity, and shake off our anxieties by reassuming our chains. But to remedy the boredom of leisure by replacing it with the boredom of labor, to seek an escape from the servitude of natural maternity through flight into the servitude of natural work, is a strange program for a movement whose goal is liberation. If God sent Eve slinking from Eden carrying the curse of childbirth—"in pain and suffering ye shall bring forth children"—he laid upon Adam no less a burden: "cursed is the ground because of you; in toil you shall eat of it all the days of your life . . . in the sweat of your brow you shall eat bread." The yoke of economic scarcity weighs on the spirit more heavily than childbirth's pains ever can.

The problem then remains. It is not a precipitate of sexism or repressive marriage, but a condition that attends the coming of post-industrial society and post-labor man and post-labor/post-maternal woman. The paralysis it can induce is no more the invention of men than it is the sectarian problem of women, albeit middle-class women are presently compelled by their circumstances to suffer it with an unwonted vengeance. It thus seems improbable that a narcissistic escape from family, flight into a romanticized world of work, will any more serve to liberate women than war serves to redress the insufficiencies of peace. Women ought to enjoy every legal and social right to work and receive equal pay for all they do. That is one thing. But to treat work as a possible solution to the dilemmas of self-realization in a world where neither productivity nor reproductivity can any longer by themselves define our identities is to forget the liberationist's point of departure. Work, like childbirth, is a necessary but no longer sufficient dimension of human identity. How peculiar that the war on nature should see the servitude of natural production as liberating but insist that natural reproduction is primarily enslaving.

As the natural roles of work and maternity are superceded by technology, we may indeed, as Robin Morgan says, find ourselves "moving beyond all known standards." But this will be a boastful war cry only among the thoughtless. As we feel more and more driven to extremes—to escapism, infantilism, narcissism and despair—by dilemmas that seem neither tractable nor tolerable, the case for prudence increases. Understandably, tragically, feminism seems too often to move instead towards escalation. Its disappointment with nature drives it into a war that dictates strategies of eradication, elimination, revolution and transformation. As its uncertainty about the future increases, its tolerance for ambivalence diminishes. This does not mean it is incapable of producing needed reforms; Firestone's extravagant program, realized tomorrow, would correct manifold injustices. As Edmund Burke noted several centuries ago, those who destroy everything are certain to remedy some grievance. But to redress by eradication is to eliminate the present and reject the past without creating a future.

"You cannot destroy the family," Leon Trotsky insisted, "you have to replace it." The alternative futures concealed by the cry *liberation!* are remarkably unclear. A few liberationists, insulated in large coastal cities, have suggested lesbian or other all-women environments for child rearing, but there seems little likelihood that such families would be any less nuclear, corrosive, or dependency-breeding than are heterosexual families at present. Deparentalized, extended family communes are a more fashionable alternative. In America at least, communes have not, however, been notably successful. Communards continue to suffer from the usual human pathologies, inflicting themselves on their comrades with the same neuroses they might have spent on marital partners. The presence of overbearing, authoritarian leaders in the more stable communes suggests that collectivities are as susceptible to domination as families, and certainly no more accommodating to liberty. Rona Jaffe reported in *New York Magazine* (in an article called "Listening in on New York's Elite Teenagers") on the plight of one young woman who had joined a commune. "Woman's liberation was very important to me . . ." she told Jaffe:

> Eight of us got together in two adjoining apartments and decided to form a sort of women's lib commune. We used to have discussions and we all tried to love each other like sisters. But after six months I realized there was only one other girl there I even liked. It was as superficial to say "I love you because you're my sister" as it is to do any of the things they're putting down. So I moved out.

One woman. One anecdote. But worth considering in a movement seeking alternative futures.

Even in other societies and other eras the record is at best checkered. Bruno Bettelheim observed in *Children of the Dream* that children raised on the kibbutz, albeit free of many of the difficulties associated with the nuclear family, pay another sort of price: they are unusually vulnerable to peer-pressure and conformism and appear inhibited in the development of precisely that individuality prized by liberationists. Margaret Mead points to

comparable patterns in the extended family kinship system of Samoa, where, she contends, "the price they pay
for their smooth, even generously gratifying system is
the failure to use special gifts, special intelligence, special intensity." Yet these may be the very traits we will
need to call on in the attempt to find meaning for our
lives in a world where nature no longer adequately
defines us. To abdicate the family at the very moment
that work ceases to provide us with clear warrants for
living seems to me to be foolish.

Emptiness is not merely, in Erik Erikson's phrase,
"the female form of perdition." It is the human form of
perdition. The French anarchist Proudhon, hardly a
stranger to arguments about liberty, acknowledged that
"fatherhood has filled an enormous emptiness in my
life." Insufficiency and the dependency that ensues from
it are inseparable from the human condition, and though
they may invite abuse and foster emotional usury, they
are implacable realities. Liberation is possible only
within their confines. That is why marriage and the
family remain crucial vehicles of liberation, providing
for healthy dependency, for a comforting interdependency that gives sanctuary to men, women and their
children in facing the encroaching void.

The tenor of these remarks is, however, primarily psychological and philosophical. Some liberationists will
rightly want to respond that it is less the interpersonal
and existential than the economic and political status of
the family that is at issue, and that whatever abstract
potential marriage may have, it has functioned histori-

cally as a vital instrument of exploitative capitalism. The
pursuit of this argument enjoins a somewhat different
line of reasoning.

III.

Feminists like Simone de Beauvoir, Juliet Mitchell or
Gail Pellet, while powerfully sensitive to psychological
dimensions of sexism, have focused also on the sociology
of the family in their writings. Following the social implications of economic determinism and class analysis,
they perceive sexism at least in part as a form of exploitation that conditions and is conditioned by capitalism.
Juliet Mitchell thus inquires in *Woman's Estate:* (a book
not so pervaded by Freud as her more recent *Psychoanalysis and Feminism*):

> What does our oppression within the family *do* to us
> women? It produces a tendency to small-mindedness,
> petty jealousy, irrational emotionality and random vio-
> lence, dependency, competitive selfishness and conserva-
> tism. These qualities are *not* the simple produce of male
> chauvinism . . . *they are the result of woman's objective condi-
> tions within the family*—itself embedded in a sexist society.

If this portrait misconceives dependency and bears a
striking resemblence to the viperous manipulator drawn
by Esther Vilar in her *The Manipulated Man*, (a book with
very different intentions from Mitchell's), it is nonetheless very firm in its insistence on the *objective* character
of woman's condition and its dependency on social rela-

tions that are presumably governed by the laws of capitalism. To assert, as I have, that women are troubled in part by a universal existential anxiety does not address the question of whether the place of women in the family is not also plagued by the relationship of capitalism to family structure.

R. D. Laing, David Cooper and their colleagues have for some time been attempting to develop a psychology of the family that illuminates individual mental illnesses in terms of social and economic pathologies. In Cooper's *The Death of the Family*, a psychological argument about the interpersonal sources of psychopathology is woven together with a sociological argument about the economic origins of sociopathology into a merciless indictment of the traditional family. "The family form of social existence," Cooper writes, "that characterizes all our institutions essentially destroys autonomous initiative . . . The family, over the last two centuries, has mediated an invasiveness into the lives of individuals that is essential to the continued operation of imperializing capitalism." Cooper's radical view, if at times obscurantist, is a typically liberationist, psychological-Marxist critique of the family. By prudently leavening psychology with what purports to be neo-Marxism, it aspires to escape the inherent conservatism of psychiatry (which is adaptation-oriented) without dispensing with its analytic insights; at the same time, it achieves the intrinsic radicalism of Marxism without becoming mired in its historicism and its neglect of individual motivation. It does not, however, evade political naiveté and anthropological innocence, for both Freudian psychology and neo-Marxism as purveyed by Cooper share these deficiencies.

I want to suggest that the coupling of capitalist exploitation with the institution of the family, albeit useful in pointing up some of the current abuses of monogamous, nuclear structures, distorts fundamentally the historical character of the family as a social institution and dangerously misunderstands the political implications of its elimination. I want to suggest, moreover, that Marx himself drew a rather different picture, and that those who urge the annihilation of the family in the name of liberation risk contributing to the creation of those anomic, atomized conditions of *Gleichschaltung* under which the most pernicious forms of political tyranny can flourish; to suggest, in sum, that the liberationist argument is effective economically and socially only because it is so defective politically.

For most of human history all social relations have been perceived as an extension of familial and kinship relations, all authority as an extension of familial authority. The clan, the tribe, even the *gens* or *Volk*, were originally but extended families; the king and monarch but fathers of extended families; vassalage but a form of kinship fealty based on natural ties. Only in recent centuries have human relations become defamilialized—public, contractual relations based on interest and governed by law replacing personal, natural relations based on familial welfare and governed by natural duty; artificial, voluntaristic and hence, dissoluble bonds replacing natural, indissoluble ones; and the separate, alienated individual replacing the organic family as the primary unit of citizenship and social structure. The rather dubious social anthropology of Engels' *Origins of the Family, Private Property and the State* is often consulted on these questions. Sir Henry Maine's *Ancient Law*, if equally dubious, is equally pertinent as a nineteenth-century source. Maine depicts the development at stake here:

> The movement of the progressive societies has been uniform in one respect. Through all its course it has been distinguished by the gradual dissolution of family dependency and the growth of individual obligation in its place. The individual is steadily substituted for the family . . . from a condition of society in which all the relations of persons are summed up in the relations of the Family, we seem to have moved [to a condition] in which all these relations arise from the free agreement of individuals.

This is no more than the evolution of the natural into the artificial polity, the corporate into the consensual state, the feudal-agrarian into the bourgeois-industrial society. The family, even today, has more in common with feudal society than with capitalist society: it is mutualist, personal and fraternal, based on ties of trust and affection rather than contract. Capitalism did not make the family; it used, abused, subordinated and tried to destroy it. For capitalism is founded on the objectification and commodization of the person (as "labor power" in Marx's language), on the alienation of the individual from natural human ties, on a celebration of interest that

sets each atomized man and woman against every other
man and woman. Listen to the voice of Marx himself, in
the *Communist Manifesto:*

> The bourgeoisie, wherever it has got the upper hand, has
> put an end to all feudal, idyllic relations. It has piteously
> torn asunder the motley feudal ties that bound man to his
> "natural superiors," and has left remaining no other
> nexus between man and man than naked self-interest,
> than callous "cash payment . . ." The bourgeoisie has torn
> away from the family its sentimental veil, and has reduced
> the family relation to a mere money relation.

The most distressing feature of liberationist arguments that fail to understand how inimical capitalism is
to the family as a form of organic community is that they
tend to support reforms which abet capitalism in its
conquest and subjugation of family structures. For example, I can think of no better way to corrupt what little
may be left of the idea of personal duty in familial relations than to introduce a public contract into marriage.
For if capitalism is, in the social realm, the contractualization of social relations, the marriage contract is simply
the bourgeoisification of the family. How better to com-
moditize interpersonal relations than to spell out supposedly permanent relationships in terms of temporary
gains and losses? How better to alienate individuals from
their identities than to treat them as business associates
in a contract entered into exclusively on the basis of
benefits received—entered into solely to enhance the private interests of the contracting parties? How better to

repress and desensitize children than to give them, as suggested by Alix Kates Shulman in a recent magazine article, what amounts to a rigid emotional labor schedule fixing the times and days when this or that parent may be asked "personal" questions?

Women have quite properly assailed men who think that the marriage license is a bill of sale legitimating their purchase of a maid or sex object—the price being the man's obligation to provide financial security. It is hardly an improvement, however, to insist that women must be sure to strike a fair bargain, must be guaranteed a just price. For this does no more than substitute a contract requiring security as the payment for sex, and protection as the price for maid service, with a contract requiring sex as the payment for sex (guaranteed orgasms for all, or your money back) and security as the price for security (equal contributions to family finances). What is really gained? The family remains a captive of private interest and acquisitiveness, marital partners persist in viewing themselves as consumers seeking the very best possible bargain (see the O'Neills' *Open Marriage*, for an unsavory example), and the narcissistic mentality (the O'Neills have a chapter called "Living For Now") so vital to the operation of consumer capitalism is given additional potency. Where once many men "bought" women, today women and men buy and consume one another like the disposable clothes, cars and hi-fi's with which they also "people" their lives. The real point of the modern marriage contract is to anticipate and provide for divorce by giving both partners a measure by which the other can be justifiably rejected when ennui, frustration and self-alienation all too predictably set in.

The strength of the traditional family in resisting the capitalist mentality has always been its firm belief in mutuality, complementarity and natural obligations that exist independently of benefits received. It is no accident that Proudhon, as a caustic critic of nineteenth-century capitalism, descried in the traditional family a life style inimical to capitalism and perfectly conducive to mutualist anarchism. If we are to cite chapter and verse, the chapter from Engels must be qualified by the verse from Maine, from Proudhon and from other sociologists of the family and community from Ferdinand Tönnies to Robert Nisbet. In Tönnies' nineteenth-century *Community and Society* the family appears as a paradigm of personal, mutualist relations and as a foil for modern, contractual, capitalist societies.

Indeed, the family is not only a foil, in its natural form, to the ravages of capitalist depersonalization, it can also be a bulwark against the encroachment of totalistic states with designs on the autonomy of individual men and women. It is fashionable among the kinds of psychoanalytic literati represented by R. D. Laing to regard the family as an establishmentarian vehicle of a conformist society. But there is another and different tradition represented by theorist-practitioners like Erich Fromm, Bruno Bettelheim and Theodore Adorno that has drawn a composite portrait of the personality type most vulnerable to mass movements and authoritarian ideologies. The research that has emerged from this tradition must engage the attention of serious liberationists, for it identifies as a potential victim of authoritarianism exactly the species of deracinated, homeless, wandering urbanite they have held up as models of liberation.

It is the person uprooted from natural ties who craves simplistic answers and total solutions, the person alienated from familial identity who capitulates most easily to the blandishments of demagogues, mass parties and virulent ideologies. The notion that ripping women and men from their natural ties and uprooting them from their social environment is tantamount to liberating them is nowhere more decisively refuted than in this body of research. Take Erich Fromm's warning in *Escape from Freedom:*

> Modern man . . . has become free from the external bonds that would prevent him from doing and thinking as he sees fit. He would be free to act according to his own will, if he knew what he wanted, thought and felt. But he does not know. He conforms to anonymous authorities and adopts a self that is not his. . . . In spite of a veneer of optimism and initiative, modern man is overcome by a profound feeling of powerlessness . . . the despair of the human automaton is fertile soil for the political purposes of fascism.

The self is not free simply because it is naked, denuded of responsibilities and obligations: it must still know itself, its nature, and if it does not it will experience its "freedom" as anomie, its liberation as anarchy, and it will flee into the safety of whatever hands will clothe it —however demeaning the garb—without a glance at the chains and manacles woven into the gray fabric. As Robert Nisbet says quite tersely (in *The Quest for Community*), when capitalism "is a sandheap of disconnected particles of humanity . . . there is nothing that can prevent the rise of centralized, omnicompetent political power." The contemporary family, sad little, fragile little community that it has become, may not do much to retard the emergence of individual powerlessness and omnicompetent political power, but surely its elimination will only hasten the coming of this dismal Fromm-Nisbet scenario. For even in its damaged form, the family stands in the way of that odious *Gleichschaltung*, that monolithic leveling process, by which totalistic power manages to divide and thus conquer women and men. Even when it seems repressive to individuality and personhood, it gives a better chance to liberty than the anomic wilderness of a market world in which humans and things—consumers and the consumed—are no longer to be distinguished.

"Despotism is never more secure than when it can keep men asunder," wrote de Tocqueville, over a century ago. But surely friends of liberty will see, then, that their cause is served by repairing the fractured structure of family life, not further dismantling it. If the family has been subjugated by capitalism, it must be restored to its natural status as a personalistic community hostile to the contractualization of human interchange. If its ties have eroded to a point where women and men no longer derive sustenance from it, where it catalyzes rather than inhibits alienation (as Cooper and other claim), then it must be reconstituted in a manner that once again permits it to nourish the maturation of autonomous, integrated beings who find liberation in intercourse with, not isolation from, their fellow beings. If it has been contractualized and ideologized nearly to death, it must be decontractualized and deideologized back into life.

The family is sick, yes. But our model ought to be restoration to health, not death of the patient. When it is healthy, the family can be a vital paradigm of permanent relationships built on uncalculating love and unneurotic commitment. The young are cynical about marriage, yes. When commitments are sealed with hypocrisy, and obligation is a code word for guilt, why should they not be? Yet again, marriage may in its healthy form be the last institution in the modern era that can still sanction a disinterested mutuality, where it is possible to give without reckoning emotional profit margins, to support without demanding contractual equity, to feel responsible without inquiring about compensation, to love without assuming passion is ephemeral.

Not that love finds very much place in the distrustful assemblages capitalism, neglect and modernity have made of modern marriage. It clearly does not. But it is in for even harder times in the anomic, alienated world that is likely to follow the Death of the Family. Many women and men have already fallen on those times—some thinking they were on the threshold of a new and freer age painted all in shades of green and watched over by a funky, immortal Aquarius. Ask them. The suburban wives who abandoned their lonely model homes for a child's dream of New York and Los Angeles that did not survive a single night in the city's second-class hotels. Ask them. The businessmen who fled to Tahiti and finding Gauguin dead had to slink home again. Ask them. The college dropouts who opted out of screwed-up families and too much making it for a Vermont commune full of screwed-up dropouts all on the make. The pretty nowhere-town football queens who turned down proposals from the boys they loved to be actresses, which turned out to mean waitresses and "rap studio" girls and worse. The happy hookers and unhappy divorcees, the graying, played-out playboys, the inseparable pairs, obdurately unmarried and bitterly childless on principle, the gay studs hating men even more than women for how much they want, how little they give . . . ask them. Ask any of them. They might have known what freedom meant once. Do they know anymore? There was not much love where they came from. Is there more now?

A simple enough lesson: the war on nature has had too many casualties. Not the liberationist's war on nature, which is well-intentioned and unrealized, but our society's war on nature with its weapons of commoditization, efficiency, contractualization and bureaucracy. That is why liberation cannot afford its inadvertent alliance with the society at large. If we cannot find a way to grow with our roots, to be free within our families, to become individuals through our polities and to acquire strength from our commitments and our love, neither women nor men—nor, least of all, human liberation—stand a chance.

But love too is a dangerous word. To many liberationists it suggests a suspect ideology, the pretty tinsel in which chauvinists have wrapped the cages in which they have imprisoned women.

IV.

Sentiment on the battlefield is almost always diversionary, and of the various sentiments love seems most out of place in the war against nature. Kate Millet has declared love "dead," Germaine Greer has labelled it a "middle-class myth," and Abby Rockefeller, afraid perhaps that it is livelier than most liberationists would wish, has stigmatized it as "both debilitating and counterrevolutionary." Chauvinism is a large and accessible target, but the "myth of love" is a more elusive and engaging foe: it camouflages sexism and obscures repression in a fog of shimmering sentiment.

Rather than attacking love outright, many feminists have followed Greer's lead and moved against it by indirection with an assault on myth, mystery and mystique. This tactic skirts the unsavory business of indicting sentiment, while enlisting the fashionable services of skepticism and technologism. Because, in our secular society, anything evoking the mythic or mystical is associated with primitive consciousness or animal unconsciousness, it is often enough to discredit an idea to qualify it adverbially or adjectively with a "myth" modifier. An ardently agnostic culture fights myth with the same vigor with which it combats nature, and although among certain young people, dropouts from the war on nature, there is a fascination with both the natural and the mystical, liberationists are mostly agnostics. Thus, Betty Friedan was able to strike a first and decisive blow against the sexism of femininity stereotypes with the very promulgation of her title *The Feminine Mystique*. And when romantics preoccupied with the psychology of love speak of the physical diffuseness and mental intensity of sexual response, Anne Koedt can dismiss them with nothing more than the phrase "the myth of vaginal orgasm." Love itself can be disposed of merely by intimating it is an unintelligible mystery, a rationalizing myth of sexist ideology.

What is most telling about the pejorative use of these terms is the implicit tribute it pays to the supposed realities of omnipotent science and to its putative capacities for liberating us from nature and nature's superstitious myths. What cannot be seen with the naked eye, what cannot be measured by scientific instruments, what is not susceptible to controlled experiment and technical replication, simply cannot be said to exist. If vaginal orgasm does not manifest itself as neural spasms visible to trained observers during laboratory intercourse, it does not exist. If femininity is not specifiable in gene-linked hereditary traits, it can only be regarded as mythical. When all is said and done, at least to Germaine Greer, kisses expressing love and kisses not expressing love "are not genuinely distinguishable." Not, at least, clinically. Lips pressing lips, tongues against teeth, a vague fish-like sucking reflex . . . kissing is kissing.

At this juncture, it looks like liberationists have forged an unfortunate alliance with crude behavioralism and pop science. In their crusade against the old myth-makers they have become victims of the new myth-makers (for at the level of ideology "myths" are simply the "truths" held by your enemies). The old myths made Man the measure of all things, thereby permitting Man's own imagination free play in giving deep, human meanings to an otherwise (that is, clinically seen) inhuman cosmos—though it did this at the risk of raising questions about whether Man meant humanity, or as it sometimes appeared, just men. The new myth avoids these sexist ambiguities by suggesting that Measure is the measure of all things, including women and men and what is to be regarded as human experience. What is, is what can be measured, what counts is what can be counted, and forget the rest—which by the pristine simplicities of the new epistemology amounts to superstitition and myth.

There is, of course, a large measure of truth in Measure: love, femininity, vaginal orgasm and all of the rich images that attend them *are* myths. They cannot be replicated or even detected by technology, they are gallingly impervious to empirical experiment, they obstinately refuse to be reduced to numbers or to neuters. They exist solely in the human imagination, in the interstices of adjacent minds linked by creativity. But then, all philosophy, all morality, all politics, all revolution, and, yes, all science are likewise wholly mythic: they are produced by and exist only in the human imagination. Civilization itself is but a concatenation of smaller myths linked together into one pervasive Myth that spreads across generations and gives to us our human identity.

What is the polity but humanity creating for itself out

of meaninglessness a common identity, an identity gene-
rated by artifice and legitimated by imagination? "Civilization," comes Yeats' somber voice ("Meru") "is hooped
together, brought under a rule, under the semblance of
peace, by manifold illusion." Measure rejects the illusions but in doing so undoes civilization. It *is* possible,
Skinner's critics notwithstanding, to get "beyond freedom and dignity" but to do so is also to get beyond
humanity, to get back to physical natures that, though
they may explain our physical behavior, cannot account
for our human identity. Likewise, it is perfectly accept-
able from the perspective of Measure to assert that there
is no such thing as vaginal orgasm; but then there is also
no such thing as clitoral orgasm. In fact, there is no such
thing as orgasm at all—understood as an emotional-
mental response of a whole personality to psychosomatic
interaction with another human being. There are only
muscle spasms and neural reactions and synaptical
events that impact in certain as yet unknown ways on
particular areas of the brain. And that is not what anybody who has ever had a sexual experience of any kind,
even under the watchful eyes of Doctors Masters and
Johnson, means by orgasm. Any more than we mean,
when we speak of a Bach violin suite, the atmospheric
vibrations produced by dragging the tail of a dead horse
across the entrails of a dead cat.

To say then that love is a myth is to say of it no more
than we say of all the ideals and illusions of civilization,
as we have fashioned it to define our unique humanity.
The human creature remains a subtle and creative being
who reads into inanimate molecules the secret of life,

who posits in a material universe the immateriality of the soul, who creates for an inchoate cosmos a cosmic Creator who in turn explains and justifies the special being of humanity, who sets soulless cells vibrating in strange oscillations that to the human heart alone are felt as the music of love. Love is not then natural in the sense that it reflects our animality; nor does it attend the magnificent solitude of divinity—the soul soaring alone above the species' mundanities. It is rather the special province of our mutuality, our uniquely human association in families and polities; it is the silken thread by which the web of civilization is held together. To think that liberation enjoins love's denial is to make war not only on nature but on civilization. It is again to misunderstand liberty, again to identify it with the anomic isolation of mechanical masturbation where meaningless orgasms can run endlessly and misanthropically on, again to regard it as an escape from mutuality rather than an acknowledgment of interdependence and the creative spirit willed interdependence can bring.

This is not to deny the darker side of myth and the dangers to civilization unreasoned mysticisms can hold. The cult of blood, the myth of Aryan superiority and the illusion of male dominance are pernicious doctrines all, in which bigotry is masked as intuition beyond the cleansing reach of discourse or reason. Norman Mailer confesses how close to fascism is the path of visceral intuition he treads in *The Prisoner of Sex.* Yet we need not be Luddite critics of industrial progress or Lawrentian advocates of the romantic pastorale to understand that our technology is increasingly subordinating our

humanity to its own technical purposes in the name of
a spurious liberation. Nor need we impeach the con-
structive demystification required in past centuries to
achieve the beginnings of economic welfare and social
justice, to perceive that the process by which we once
removed burdensome superstitions is now being employed to denude women and men of their very
humanity. The man overburdened by unnecessary layers of confining clothes may do well to strip some of
them away; but this is not a warrant for the normative
principle "Strip!" for there will come a time, perhaps by
the time he is down to his underwear, and certainly
when he reaches his epidermis, when the once-sensible
principle becomes pointless, counterproductive, and
finally self-destructive.

In an age of unreason and superstition a people can
become slave to their myths, and freedom will indeed
mean the loosening of social structures and the substitu-
tion of rationality for personalism and its blood mysteries. The condition of our age suffers other afflictions,
however. We have become slaves to our secularism, impotent vassals of our "progressive" skepticism; the
science with which we vanquished superstition and con-
quered nature has in turn become our own sovereign
master. In the eighteenth century, had he held the same
views (which seems unlikely), Mailer would have appeared as a Jesuit reactionary fighting to preserve a mori-
bund power structure that used mythology as an instrument of legitimizing self-preservation. But today he is a
heretical believer at war with a religiously atheistic society, a revolutionary who would use myth to smash the

complacent materialism that is at the very center of the American system of power.

From the prison of traditional and primitive society, the first step to liberation of any kind was the elimination of cultural bars and social locks, an elimination associated historically with the rationalization and modernization of society. But once "free," the self seeking realization in individual women and men discovers how very small a step it has taken; it may even realize that the key to its true emancipation lies back in the jail of its past where an unthought kinship provided answers to troublesome questions that individual liberation only exacerbates. Very much as the teenage rebel against parental authority and familial identity may nonetheless look with a certain nostalgia on the childhood he has rejected. This does not mean that the partially liberated, modern self ought to abandon reason, overthrow the new god science, and leap headlong back into the mindless comforts of primitive collectivity and its involuntary (ascriptive) identities. Any more than the rebel can be rescued from the perils of adolescent independence by regressing into infancy.

The problem with those who make war on nature is that they mistake adolescence for maturity, they confound its indiscriminate rebelliousness with final liberation, and they confuse the heady transience of sudden independence with the far more demanding permanence of mature self-fulfillment. They misunderstand liberty, and so cannot really light our way to liberation. Wherever they see nature they turn and run in the other direction, on the premise that liberty always lies in the other direction. If one were to say that liberty had something to do with facing towards, facing up to nature—acknowledging its powers while shaping its impact—the war on nature would have to be abandoned. To put an end to so unproductive and diverting a battle would, I believe, be an important step in liberating feminism. Once liberated from the ideological baggage of the society's establishment, and clear about the interdependence of liberty and nature, it would be in a position to engage the real foes of liberation: the materialists and bureaucrats and interest-mongers and technocrats and behavioralists and ideologues and hedonists and bigots who together conspire to annihilate our human identity by destroying family mutualism, committed love, and the just polity.

How intransigent these foes can be is all too well demonstrated by the character of the response to the liberationist movement. It has fought on behalf of "nature" with an ardor no less defiant than that of the liberationists, but with less cause, less justification, and less candor. It misunderstands nature far more completely than the liberationists misconceive liberty, and with far more dangerous consequences. Before, then, I can suggest how it might be possible to mediate between nature and liberation with peace terms that do justice both to our nature and our aspirations, I must digress to comment briefly on the reaction to feminism. It has, with several important exceptions, been a disgrace. Were I not wholly persuaded that the war was being fought on the wrong ground over the wrong issues, the character of the arguments advanced on behalf of those defending nature's good name would have long since driven me into the arms of the liberationists.

3

The War on Liberation, or Misunderstanding Nature

COMING TO THE LITERATURE AND IDEOLOGY that has sprung up around the citadel of nature in reaction to radical feminism is rather like—after tiring of the rhetoric of the French Revolutionaries—being exposed to the speeches of Louis XVI at his trial: it gives a new liveliness to feminist ideas and a new urgency to their programs. It tends to excuse their excesses and justify their rhetoric, for it suggests that almost anything is preferable to the status quo and the querulous legitimations of its defenders. Because my intent is to provide an alternative perspective for liberation, I cannot succumb to the temptation to use the arguments of the naturalist reaction as a motivation, without further ado, to join the revolution. But the temptation ought to be noted, for if not the most cerebral it is one of the more telling arguments that can be made on behalf of feminism.

The claims of the naturalists are manifold and often mutually inconsistent. Nonetheless, as with the feminists, their premises reduce to several fundamental propositions that can be said, together, to define their perspective. Two claims are paramount: that

— there is no problem; or, in its aggressive variation, that the problem is not *femininity* and its abuse but feminism and *its* abuses;

and, covering all bets as it were, that

— even if there is a problem, it must be regarded as an integral feature of our condition: natural, inevitable, irremediable, and indeed desirable.

The first claim suggests nothing ought to be done and the second that nothing can be done. Together they constitute a position on women rather like the one held by the authority on ghosts who insisted he neither believed in spirits nor feared them: unassailable and untenable. The position is quite common with "men in the street." The man who beats his wife thus says, "I never touched her, and besides she asked for it"; or the discriminatory employer boasts, "I pay all my workers the same, and anyway the girls don't need as much with their husbands working"; or the Little League official declares, "We let everyone play baseball, only girls can't so we don't let them."

Naturalist writers, being men in the street with typewriters in the attic, purvey the same views. George Gilder *(Sexual Suicide)* thus chides feminists for their "whole array of nostrums designed to emancipate us."

"From what?" he queries, for to him "all the clichés of our social crisis spring from, or reflect and reinforce, a fundamental deformation of sexuality." Feminism, not sexism, is the problem. Norman Mailer, too magical a writer to count strictly as a naturalist—or as an ideologue of any stripe—nonetheless manages in *The Prisoner of Sex* to make feminism's intolerance for the "fragility" of men (also appealed to by Esther Vilar, Steven Goldberg and countless others who seem determined to conceal the realities of male power in male inadequacy) the leading pathology of our time, thereby diverting attention from the condition of women to the condition of men. A great deal of naturalism's rhetoric seems to reduce to the apolitical psychic cry, "Give me back my mommy and to hell with justice." Even Midge Dechter *(The New Chastity and Other Arguments Against Woman's Liberation)*, who cannot be classified as a naturalist at all since she thinks women are plagued not by nature's bonds but society's excessive freedoms, seems to suggest that the problem is in the heads of spoiled women rather than in the body politic—only to conclude that for extravagantly liberated women they certainly are behaving like frightened serfs.

The assault on liberation thus tries to have it both ways: women have no problem and besides it is their own fault. In order to treat intelligently with naturalism, however, the claims need to be separated—though on purely logical grounds, the claim that the problem is irremediable and largely of woman's own making would seem to relieve me of responsibility for refuting the claim that there is no problem at all.

I.

There is, of course, a problem. And it is not, as the
"outside agitator" variation on the naturalist theme has
it, the problem that troublemakers and other sociopathic
malcontents are creating spurious anxieties among otherwise docile populations of loving wives and content
mothers. This variation is so obvious an evasion, so frequently and futilely employed a diversion by other can-
tankerous reactionaries opposing other just revolutions,
that it hardly merits consideration. Indeed, it has the
dubious virtue of being irrefutable, since what normally
counts as evidence for injustice equally well counts as
evidence for outside agitation. In the South during the
integration struggle, for every grievance there was an
uppity nigger, for every act of resistance a Northern
agitator spreading lies, for every attempt at change a big
city reporter trying to stir up sensational headlines. You
simply cannot beat that game. Fortunately, it cannot be
won either. The grievances, when real, outlive the
fiction of agitators, and the indignation, when noble, is
intensified by attempts to discredit it.

Nor is the problem, I have argued in the previous
section, the oppressive enslavement of women—a construction which, in claiming too much, almost guaran-
tees that too little will be done. For it misses the true
dimensions of our dilemma and plays into the hands of
its caricaturists by overdrawing itself so excessively. But
the problem is there. It arises at every turning. It is a
problem of injustice, discrimination and inequality at a
level of mundanity that enhances rather than diminishes

its pervasiveness and urgency. Housewives are committing suicide. That is the problem. Educated women cannot find jobs. That is the problem. The physical and psychological demands of having babies can no longer occupy a lifetime. That is the problem. Marriages that once had to survive only (say) twenty years in a stable society now are supposed to last (say) fifty in an unstable society. That too is the problem. Women will no longer tolerate a hypocritical promiscuity that permits adolescent infidelity to charade as "male fragility." Or a hypocritical maternalism that leaves children with women who want custody no more than their departing husbands. And what, then, of the children—victims of their parents' new-found authenticity? These too are problems.

Whatever naturalists contend, women know with a certainty words cannot cheat them of that being a woman can in this society in this time be a liability—an obstacle to becoming a person, an impediment to achieving equal rights, a barrier to self-realization. Not always; not inevitably; not irremediably; but too often, too ineluctably; too unprotestingly. These are problems too real to be dismissed. That observers as sensitive to the human predicament as Mailer and Dechter should be oblivious to them is shocking. But then aesthetic sensibility and justice have never been the match the poets hoped for. As for the rest of the naturalists, their oblivion is merely predictable. From George Gilder's propitious half-truths in defense of social structure and family to Wallace Reyburn's Goebbel's-quoting whole-lies flailing *The Inferior Sex* (the title is the most generous thing he says

of women), naturalism has been too busy nursing the
wounds it brought with it into battle to pay much attention to what the enemy claimed to be fighting for.

Nevertheless, under pressure, naturalists are willing
enough to abandon their hollow cry "all's well!" It is
an exposed position from which they generally expect
to have to fall back. The redoubt is necessity: the claim
that it is nature which has cast men and women into
the roles they play, and nature that will not permit
them to evade their animal destinies. Like it or not, the
critical brief reads, nature is master. Naturalists, of
course, tend to like it. A few turncoats like Ashley
Montagu *(The Natural Superiority of Women)* and Esther
Vilar *(The Manipulated Man)* because they think nature
has given women the upper hand anyway—the rest, because it legitimates the status quo (Steven Goldberg in
The Inevitability of Patriarchy) or even justifies retrogres-
sion (George Gilder's spirited defense of the natural
family gradually turns into a disspiriting assault on
gun-control, birth control [Mailer's nemesis as well],
busing and the war on poverty). But like it or despise
it, nature is supreme. To spurn it, naturalists conclude,
can only augment human grief. The anxieties and
dilemmas of the present time are themselves, in the
naturalist view, but a taste of the revenge nature plans
to take on the liberationists and their vain conceits—as
if nature were the Almighty driving us from Eden for
our vainglorious aspirations to an unnatural freedom,
(whereas nature, in truth, is the desert to which the
species was sent packing from Eden).

II.

This second claim promulgating the inevitability of the natural in human affairs suffers from three fundamental deficiencies that render it untenable as an account of the natural condition, and fallacious as an account of the limiting conditions on what our natural possibilities may be. These three errors are inseparable from naturalism's defining refusal to recognize the human condition as distinct from the natural condition, and inseparable from its principled denial of the potentialities of freedom and personhood in the civilized polity. Because naturalism is, in this sense, synonymous with its deficiencies, it cannot survive their exposure. As their poverty reveals its bankruptcy, so their elimination entails its downfall. No more is required, then, in this section, than the treatment of these three errors.

The three are, in preliminary summation, the error of thinking that the history of civilization as a history of rising consciousness, increasing control over nature and expanding horizons of human possibility has had no impact on nature and its stern necessities—what can be identified as naturalism's *ahistoricity;* the conjunctive error of confounding an abstract, ahistorical "natural" condition with the real (and equally "natural" in the generic sense) condition of women and men in advanced industrial societies in the late twentieth century—what we can call naturalism's abstract *apoliticity;* and the philosophical error (akin to what is known in the formal literature as the naturalistic fallacy) of believing that

moral standards of any kind whatsoever can be derived
from or gain their sustaining normative power from
"natural" descriptions of any kind whatsoever—what
amounts to naturalism's *amoralism*.

These sweeping errors arise out of and are reinforced
by naturalism's studied selectivity in choosing academic
allies suitable to its quintessential premise: that human
beings are animals and ought to be studied accordingly.
Biology, physiology, and certain deterministic schools of
psychology, anthropology and ethology are consulted;
but history is ignored—hence the neglect of our condition's changeability; political sociology is slighted—
hence, the oblviousness to the concrete political and social dilemmas of modern women; and morals and politics, when they are not being reduced to psychology and
biology, are passed over—hence, the attempt to read
moral lessons on how we ought to live out of nature's
textbook on how animals putatively do live. With history, sociology, ethics and political theory safely out of
the way, naturalists need not even bother to dismiss
equality, freedom or personhood. The terms simply do
not arise as part of ethology, the natural study of our
species' nature, for they are distinctively moral, political
and social concepts intelligible only within the humanizing confines of civilized polities. Naked apes cannot be
"free" in any relevant political or moral sense, nor can
dominant males and "imperial animals" be persons.
Moral speech is the language of the polity, the province
of beings who achieve uniqueness with the very contriv-
ances through which they affect to be unique. The
refusal of naturalists to think in the deepest sense *politi-*

cally—which is to say, both historically and morally as well—is, as I have argued from the opening pages of this book, at the root of their error.

The first error, ahistoricity, like each of the other two, is an error both of omission and of commission. Omitting history, it commits every conceivable error of abstraction, timelessness and anachronism. Staring fixedly at man's aggressive penis and the invisible hormones that fuel that instrument's timeless campaigns of conquest, and at woman's hidden womb that enjoins an eternity of passive maternity, naturalists fail to notice the clothes with which history has muted the sharp contours of human sexuality and mitigated the force of its obliging drives. Asking naturalists about the impact of history on nature is very much like asking the pop-eyed pornographer habituated to undressing women with his imagination to comment on fashion. At best he will perceive in clothes salacious bulges and suggestive hollows. George Gilder, on his way to undressing the species, thus perceives in society's garb only the repressed curves of natural women and natural men—penises strapped down by the codpiece of law to preserve us from their havoc, bellies decorated by petticoats of marriage to remind us of our natural duties to reproduction and species survival.

If history is taken seriously, however, the malleability of nature—our own natures—in response to the shaping forces of human artifice cannot be so easily evaded. Human history has permitted more than an expression of our nature: it has permitted a redefinition. The laws by which it contained us have been the instruments of our

emancipation. And in our defiance of nature, of the animality from which we indisputedly sprang, we have discovered our unique humanity. As Rousseau, a better
friend to nature than many of its contemporary proponents, writes in *The Social Contract:*

> The passage from the state of nature to the civil state
> produces a very remarkable change in man, by substitut-
> ing justice for instinct in his conduct, and giving his ac-
> tions the morality they had formerly lacked. Then only,
> when the voice of duty takes the place of physical impulse
> and right of appetite, does man, who so far had considered
> only himself, find that he is forced to act on different
> principles, and to consult his reason before listening to his
> inclinations.

Our evolution as political beings took man from nature
and "instead of a stupid and unimaginative animal, made
him an intelligent and truly human being." Earth-buried
roots spawned air-breathing leaves—the trunk was civilization. This is no Rousseauian conceit. Hegel, Marx,
Weber and scores of lesser theorists have rehearsed the
theme on their own particular stage. History, in Hegel's
stunning phrase, is the march of freedom in the world.
The realm of freedom, of a history we will make for
ourselves, is for Engels the end of history as we know it,
the end of the history made for us by nature and its yoke
of economic scarcity.

The debate need not be carried on, however, at the
level of world-historical abstractions favored by theorists. The reality is as mundane as what has happened to

hunger, as concrete as the historical struggle against sickness. Hunger and disease have, after all, been two of nature's least tractable masters, compelling us into life-long labor while simultaneously making long life a privilege few could expect to enjoy. Yet labor productivity and scientific medicine, each born of consciousness seizing upon and molding the natural forces impinging upon us, have gradually loosened the grip of our stomachs upon our lives, and stayed the hand of death with increasing stubbornness.

To argue, as naturalists do, that we are by *nature* sexual animals driven by forces which society can at best only disguise, is to say we are by nature famished lepers afflicted with sicknesses that nutrition, good health and longevity can only camouflage. The point is, historically speaking, the "disguise" is more significant, more "natural," than the condition it remedies or mitigates or satisfies. The history of our indenture to natural reproduction has much in common with the history of our subservience to hunger and disease. The same civilizing forces of science, organization and law that have been responsible for our emancipation from them, have eased our reproductive serfdom. It is very well for George Gilder to yearn for a stable nuclear family sanctuary for the distraught bachelors with whom he apparently identifies, and it is even appealing to listen to Norman Mailer celebrate the cosmic miracle of conception—but they both speak from the prudent perspective of a society that has reproduction under control. "Good fucks make good babies" is Mailer's law, his tribute to raunchy spirituality.

But nature's law is raunchier, uglier: "Fucks make babies, babies, babies and more babies ... and death takes them away as fast as fucks make them." That is nature's law. And it is not Mailer's law but nature's law that enslaves the Punjab mother, with her two stillbirths, seven dead infants and nine living children crowding into her life, gnawing away at her viscera, leaving her no gift but helplessness and fear. Yes, the man with a full stomach can look to other meanings for his life than mere survival—he may even meditate, over brandy and coffee, on the splendid necessities by which King Nature invests our lives with meanings wholly natural. But in his meditation he ought not to condemn the woman who perceives in medicine an avenue to other meanings in her life than reproduction, who thinks of history as the liberating sequence of arduous discoveries by which maternity finally became a choice. A full womb, like a full stomach, can release the spirit and prompt the imagination to a quest for creative personhood. History has made it possible for women to fill their wombs by choice without filling their lives with dying infants—to be mothers without surrendering the right to be persons. To the degree that the liberation movement hopes to institutionalize these welcome changes, it deserves far better from the naturalists than it gets.

The real cost of this first error of ahistoricity is the second still graver error of apoliticity. The cataracts afflicting naturalism's historical vision produce a severe astigmatism when naturalists come to look at woman's present condition. George Gilder writes "the maternal feeling is the root of the human community," civilization being a device by which men are made to "subordinate their sexual rhythms to extended female perspectives." For Steven Goldberg "the hormonal renders the future inevitable." Norman Mailer is prepared to "speak of men and women as the poles of the universe, the universal Yang and Yin, to offer views of the Creation such abstract lands as seed and womb, vision and firmament, fire up a skyworks of sermon and paean to the incontestible mystery that women are flesh of the Mystery more than men." And Midge Dechter draws the dreadful conclusion: "There is no more radical nor desperately nihilistic statement to issue from the lips of humans than that there are no necessary differences between the sexes. For such differences both issue in and constitute . . . the continuation of life on earth." But continuation for what? What is the human mission of the species other than replicating itself endlessly? The tocsin sounds: if women are wombs and wombs are destiny, then woe the women who aspire to wombless personhood! If good fucks make good babies, pray for the women who aspire to more than fucking and babies, for they risk losing their souls—a cervical organ, the naturalists appear to believe, connecting the uterus to the vagina. But what for? The question of meaning cannot be postponed forever from mother to child. The justification for producing new beings is that we find meaning in our own lives that we presume our children too will discover.

What then in reality is the condition of women? Yes, they make love, they fuck, conceive and bear as ever before. But has history taken us no farther? The hungry man, it is true, knows no other aspiration than eating,

and if, upon eating, he were to die, he might well be
defined quintessentially as a "natually eating animal"
whose identity arises out of the mysteries of ingestion.
Women, for millenia, have been defined and defined
themselves as "naturally childbearing animals," and understood the meaning of their lives accordingly. And
why not? Women have quite literally spent most of human history having babies and then dying—an enterprise demanding ceaseless fortitude in centuries when
the fecundity of the womb was surpassed only by the
voraciousness of death. For all its bluff omnipotence,
nature was an inefficient master. It required women to
bring forth ten children merely to salvage two or three
from the mortal ravages of sickness and malnutrition.
Indeed, nature's tyranny lay precisely in its inefficiency:
maternity was destiny because nature's sloppy formula
made a lifelong project of what ought to have taken only
a few years.

The history of human civilization has to a large extent
been the history of our race's attempt to compensate and
overcome not nature but nature's appalling wasteful-
ness, its wanton inefficiency. The costs of that inefficiency to individual women and men were centuries of
slavery and suffering—sixteen hour days of body-
wrenching toil merely to feed ourselves, mothers and
children decimated at gruesome rates merely to replen-
ish our stock. But with agriculture we rationalized the
uncertain gifts of the soil, with tools we multiplied the
strengths and skills of deficient bodies, with institutions
and collective endeavor we compensated the insufficiency of our individuality. And finally, only recently,

with education and medicine, we have overcome the costly inefficiencies and careless slavery of reproduction.

That is not to say we need no longer reproduce, Dechter's extravagant fears notwithstanding, any more than agriculture suggests we need no longer eat. It does mean that what once was nature's whim is now woman's will, what once was given now can be chosen. Birth control does not mean no babies, it means babies when they are wanted and needed. Medicine does not interdict the cycle of reproduction, but it does permit two births to produce two healthy humans and thereby puts an end to nature's indifferent arithmetic. Most significantly of all, these developments permit women to see themselves as something more than reproducing animals; not *other* than—that is the fallacy of liberationism—but *more* than that. This is the reality of woman's modern condition. The problem is that attitudes and institutions have not yet fully adjusted to reality. And the naturalists have not yet even begun to adjust.

All of Gilder's biological paeans, all of Mailer's mystery-drawn embellishments of transcendent wombs, all Goldberg's assurances that maternity *is* power (properly understood) are atavistic tributes to a version of womanhood that has passed away in modern industrial societies —rationalizations, glorifications, guilty deifications of a slavery women in fact no longer bear. The naturalist imagination (which is an ironic self-contradiction since naturalism denies creative consciousness) conjures inspiring earth mothers, pregnant goddesses whose mouths are vaginas and whose eyes are gleaming ovaries, whose breasts carry centuries of nurture in cloud-soft

hillocks topped with roses . . . and in the ecstasy of their
visions, real women living in the middle 1970s disappear.
Naturalist writers, like the rest of us, presumably are
surrounded by real women—mothers, wives, sisters,
daughters—but in the glitter of their dazzled visions real
women are not easily descried. A male naturalist (though
some are women) scans the horizon for distant feminists,
an imagined enemy with breasts turned to battering
rams and vaginas sealed off with barbed wire, but his
mother passes by unnoticed.

And yet she is there, remembered by him, if she is
lucky, if at all, as a pillowed fortress against the demons
of childhood, an encouraging, selfless smile smoothing
the paths to maturation. Selfless smile: fixed smile, soulless smile. For she is fifty, and were her son to stare into
her eyes he would discover a vexing wonderment about
what it all is supposed to mean now that the children are
grown, dad buried, and widowed solitude the only prospect in a life certain to outspan dignity. She reassured
herself always that her children justified her life, persuaded herself that maternity would fill the expanding
void where a soul should have been—and she hoped
vaguely that death would claim her before truth. Now,
photos, memories, grandchildren across a continent, hos-
pitals, telephone calls and finally some Forgotten Acres
rest home that will provoke a comforting senility: these
will be the graying milestones of the rest of her life.
Because she is a woman beyond the age of maternity
without a capacity for personhood, because the miracle
of science has kept her alive when nature has stopped
telling her what for, because she has outlived, will out-

live by decades, the womb that was supposed to define her.

Then there is our generic naturalist's sister, thirty-two, mother of three, still married, ostensibly content. Her womb is alive, vibrant, hoping if wombs can hope for the coming of more wriggling invaders and still another miracle of conception. But she doesn't want any more babies. Three is already embarrassing in a wealthy society in which an only child consumes the equivalent in resources of what would satisfy a dozen Bengalis or Ik. And besides, she has known and savored the maternal experience and looks for other forms of self-expression. She doesn't want to leave her family, but she does want a job. She loves her husband enough to know she cannot live through him or steal from him the second shadow of his identity. She remembers having brought one of her own from college into the marriage, but she has misplaced it. It has slipped behind the washing machine, or fallen behind the refrigerator; or perhaps she inadvertently traded it in for the new pram. It is gone, that much she knows. And she wants it back. But what job? It's been a dozen years since college and she majored in English. English! And her competitors are young women with an aggressiveness she can better admire than imitate. And the men who interview her seem to think she must be on the make, and they won't train her and won't offer a decent salary anyway, and her husband is beginning to complain that she is spending more time looking for work than most women do working and . . . and . . . what is she to do? Go back to school? With all those *eighteen-year olds?* Move out—just for a while?

She has to do something: too many of her friends are
seeing lawyers, or on the bottle, or in the hospital or
toying with suicide. If only she could find herself again,
find that young person who wanted babies and a home
but knew too that there was more to life than the satisfaction of sexuality and the fulfillment of maternity. But she
is unlikely to. The society makes it easier to take a lover
than to take a job, easier to spoil her marriage than spoil
the illusions of homemaking, easier to destroy herself
than find herself.

And the naturalist's daughter: nineteen, torn between
cashing in on or dropping out of a society that is forebod-
ing either way, liking but hardly trusting men, addicted
to sex but skeptical of love. Asking with her ambivalence
for guidance her instincts cannot give her (babies hardly
answer her questions) and the society seems incapable of
offering. She is wise enough to know living alone, a room
of her own, is not liberation, but she knows too that there
will be no escape for her generation back into blind
maternity, no drowning of consciousness in childbirth.
She is not at all sure of what the answers are, but she
demands the right to seek them and the means of finding
them: she thus demands power, income, status—the
privileges her father insists are mere compensations for
his self-servingly self-belittling biological inferiority.
She is a little frightening, for she asks a great deal and
seems unaware of the costs. When warned of how much
power exacts and how little it gives she replies: Let me
have some and I will tell you if that is so. She is going
to make a great many mistakes, but she will not pine her

way to senility with the dazed wonderment of her grandmother.

These are the real women. They are not necessarily feminists, but feminists have looked into their faces (sometimes in mirrors) and recognized that something must be done. Their situations are not dramatic, they are not oppressed or enslaved. But their situations are real enough—painful, frustrating, inequitable, unfair. To throw nature at them, shouting that if they would open their legs they could shut their mouths, is to forget that history and civilization have made nature too little. It still gives much, but it is no longer enough. Most women acknowledge nature, recognize how deeply satisfying maternity can be. They do not need lessons in childbirth from male keepers of the Eternal Womb. They know enough to understand that nature's insufficiency is both a problem and an opportunity. A problem because it encumbers women with difficult choices at the same moment it withdraws its enforcing guidelines (some of the complications of which are intelligently discussed by Midge Dechter); but it is also an opportunity in that it opens up possibilities of self-determination and creativity hitherto precluded by nature's monstrous inefficiencies.

It is understandable, given naturalism's apoliticity, that these realities go mostly unperceived. Naturalists are forever urging us to choose in favor of options that do not exist, to preserve status quos that have long since disappeared. They speak of the damage that feminism is doing to the family as if capitalism had not already ravaged it; they speak of the need to socialize wayward ghetto males into stable families as if the society at large was healthy. They have much in common with the anti-abortionists who debate as if the issue were whether to have babies or have abortions. Big-city doctors know better. The only real question is whether we are to have safe, legal, planned abortions linked with contraceptive education programs or to continue having unsafe, illegal abortions that kill and maim the least fortunate young women—many under sixteen years old. It is the same with maternity. Disruptive feminists are not corrupting the pleasure and meaning women find in marriage and the family. On the contrary, the insufficiency of pleasure and incompleteness of meaning derived from modern motherhood are creating disruptive feminists. The painful struggle for personhood that follows in the wake of successful civilizations and the delegitimation of natural necessity they make possible cannot be wished away. Politics and morals must now be employed to discover and to choose values and meanings nature once provided.

In this there is absolutely no difference between men and women. This is not, as Dechter seems to think, to deny sexual differentiation, but to accept that as persons faced with the burdens and possibilities of discovering our own meanings and shaping our own destinies with the help, but no longer the deciding authority, of nature, our differences are nil. As members of the human polity and aspirers to justice and to self-determination we are alike.

This suggests the paramount need for political and

moral discourse, a need to which naturalists no less than liberationists seem inured. Anyone who has tried to pursue Mailer trembling down pathways to ecstacy, or followed Goldberg and Gilder into their pop ethological miocenes where they claim to have recovered the Meaning of Life; anyone accompanying Esther Vilar into her debased little world of cynicism more blustering than blistering for all her studied blasphemies; anyone, in other words, who has spent time with the naturalists will have noticed a striking hiatus in their language. Terms like justice, obligation, morality, responsibility, equity, legality, self-determinism, creativity and liberty are hardly ever employed, the rational discourse such terms ought to enjoin never entered upon.

Even the more accessible obverse side of politics where notions of power, rank, privilege and status can be found is generally shunned. Vilar is mesmerized by manipulation and others like Gilder and Mailer try to invest classic female strengths with overtones of sovereignty, as if to suggest that prudent females allow men their political fun and games since women hold the real strings (that hook up, inconspicuously, to certain lower abdominal organs). This tactic, belied straight away by the ardor with which naturalists cling to the real trappings of power—money, jobs, high office—is as transparent as the tactic of the warden who tries to persuade his prisoners that, considering the leisure they enjoy and state support they exploit, they are the ones who exercise the *real* privileges of freedom. In fact, I cannot think of a single tract written against liberation that attempts a serious discussion of economics, status, privilege or power. Much less justice or equity. "What is natural?" is never confronted with the query, "What is right?" "What are the consequences of our biological differentiation?" is never parried with, "and what are the consequences of our common personhood?" Nature's prescriptions are manifold: it makes us murderous, aggressive, famished, diffident, leperous, creative, hungry and reproductive. What sort of creatures, then, do we choose to be when civilization pries loose the grip of nature enough to allow some movement? These are questions quite beyond the naturalist perspective, questions that reveal naturalism's third and most perilous error.

Naturalism's incapacity to generate an adequate ethic is founded on two deficiencies, both of which are mixed up in the so-called naturalistic fallacy. They each reflect on the ambivalence of the idea of nature. First, nobody can in fact agree on precisely what it is that is "natural." Second, even if consensus is stipulated, a clear description of what is natural can have, by definition, no normative force in moral argument. In brief, we do not know what human nature is and if we did it would not and could not give us the standards by which we judge that nature and how it is to be modified in the name of our ideals. In this rather perplexing confusion, naturalists essaying to make some alleged idea of nature the basis for our institutional ideals are only sharing in the faults of the more general school to which their mode of discourse belongs: that of ethology, which sees in our natural species' origins clues to our human future.

This approach is much older even than Darwin: it can be traced back to hedonists and animal interest theorists like Bentham, Hobbes and, much earlier, Thrasymachus as depicted in Plato's *Republic*. But its recent vogue among the general public is probably no older than Robert Ardrey's *African Genesis*, first published in 1961. Ardrey sounded the note with which all later naturalist writings were to try to achieve resonance when he wrote at the beginning of the chapter he called "The New Enlightenment:"

> In neither bankruptcy nor bastardy did we face our long beginnings. Man's line is legitimate. Our ancestry is firmly rooted in the animal world, and to its subtle, antique ways our hearts are yet pledged ... man is a fraction of the animal world. Our history is an afterthought, no more, tacked onto an infinite calender. We are not so unique as we should like to believe. And if man in a time of need seeks deeper knowledge concerning himself, then he must explore those animal horizons from which we have made our quick little march.

All of naturalism's themes are there: humankind's essential animality, its inevitable bondage to its natural origins, the irrelevance of human history and its civilized precipitates, and nature's usefulness as a source of guidelines in a troubled age.

Since the publication of *African Genesis*, Konrad Lorenz has rooted human aggression in animal nature *(On Aggression)*, Ardrey himself has explored the roots of property, competition and war in animal territoriality *(The Territorial Imperative)*, and Lionel Tiger has constructed an anthropological genealogy of male bonding

(Men In Groups) and, with Robin Fox, tried to weld biology and anthropology into a complete ethology of human behavior *(The Imperial Animal)*. Tiger and Fox are
quick to note that "this is not a matter of seeking attrac-
tive analogies between human and animal ways, but of
insisting that we are animals still and that things that are
true for the rest of nature hold true for us too." Men as
beasts, period. No wonder that war, aggression, and ex-
clusivity rank so high (though objective non-humans
might wonder if animals were not in fact getting the
worst of the comparison, given the ethologist's an-
thropomorphic tendency to read back into animal nature
our species' most uniquely human and uniquely perverse evils).

With the credentials of ethological argument well established, and its voguishness in a science-struck society
assured, it was, as it were, a natural for the naturalists
seeking to discredit liberation. If weaponry and territoriality (Ardrey), aggression and war (Lorenz), and fraternal bonding (Tiger) could all be regarded as "natural"
and for the most part "inevitable," then surely it could
be argued that patriarchy (Steven Goldberg), female
quiescence (George Gilder), and continuous conception
(Norman Mailer) are equally "natural" and "inevitable."
If respectable anthropologists like Tiger could assert
that man "is programmed [by nature, this is not B.F.
Skinner!] to behave in certain ways" and that "if he
chooses to behave otherwise, then he must do so with as
much hope of success as those who ignore the basic
physical laws," surely it was no less respectable to assert

that male dominion and female passivity were equally "programmed" and that to lure women from the kitchens and nurseries where nature had carefully left them would be tampering with immutable natural laws.

Unfortunately, in stealing ethology's mode of argument, the naturalists stole its deficiencies as well. Like the poor bear who made off with the wasps' nest, naturalists seem not to realize that the bees who torment them came with the honey they borrowed. Nature has always been a problematic standard; its potentiality as a source of moral and political norms has been compromised by the confusion and disagreement that surrounds its "true" character. Participants in the prolonged social contract tradition who hoped to derive from a description of man's "natural condition" justification for his political obligations had, for example, never reached a consensus on the nature of nature. To Hobbes, men were naturally in a state of permanent war of all against all, wasting away, in useless conflict, lives that were "solitary, poor, nasty, brutish and short." Yet for Locke, mankind's natural condition was one of "Peace, good will, mutual assistance, and preservation." Evolutionary theorists have been no more in accord. Darwin identified the natural state and its laws of species preservation with competition and conflict between species; Prince Kropotkin (as a biologist in his *Mutual Aid*) insisted, to the contrary, that evolution's instrument was natural mutualism and cooperation within species. Recent ethologists continue to disagree. There is a good deal of talk about imperiousness and aggressiveness, but territoriality as a natural concept has defensive overtones and male bonding emphasizes natural gregariousness rather than natural individuality.

Among naturalists appealing to the natural conditions of our animal sexuality, the discord persists. George Gilder thinks "civilization evolved through the subordination of male sexual patterns—the short term cycles of tension and release—to the long term female patterns," and could presumably appeal to Freud's *Civilization and Its Discontents* for support. Yet Mary Jane Sherfy, a liberationist deploying naturalist strategies, concludes from her "natural" evidence that "the rise of modern civilization . . . was contingent on the suppression of the inordinate cyclic drives of women." Take your choice: women invent civilization to tame men's sexual insatiability or men invent civilization to tame women's sexual insatiability. Both propositions are labelled "natural," both are derived from the supposed facts of biology and anthropology. And so, while Steven Goldberg and Wallace Reyburn keep busy promoting the "natural" superiority of men, Ashley Montagu and, in her own perverse way, Esther Vilar, sell books proclaiming the "natural" superiority of women.

What is perhaps silliest about this irresoluble debate is that its resolution, even were it possible, would make no difference whatever to the moral and political dilemmas we face. There is a logical and a psychological hiatus between what nature makes us and what we make of ourselves, between description and prescription. Let us assume for a moment that the chemical analysis of DNA, the physiological manifestations of testosterone, and the evidence drawn from anthropology all pointed to a single conclusion: that the male animal *homo sapiens* was by nature an incorrigible killer. Would that be a basis on which to suspend the commandment "thou shalt not kill"? or to organize institutions in ways that facilitate murder? or plan our futures around death? Obviously not. Moral dicta are necessarily in tension with what comes "naturally." We do not require a commandment exhorting us to eat or prescribing selfishness. These "come naturally" and it is the object of morals to control what comes naturally in the name of the transnatural or the supernatural.

It is precisely because humans do kill "naturally," that ethics and law exist—a tribute to the stand taken by our intentions, our aspirations and our ideals against the "natural" givens with which animality saddles us. To argue that morals derive from "nature" in anything like this sense, is really to reduce the moral to the descriptive, to substitute power for morality. Once the rhetoric is cleared away, the argument against social equality for men and women and against the possibilities of human liberation reduce to the familiar immoralism of "might makes right." Nature endowed men with clubs with which, in turn, men make and enforce laws and morals. So much for justice. Or freedom. Were the naturalists true to their logic, they would have to suggest that the sick and the weak and the old and the infirm *among males* be relegated to the second class citizenship that is the just desert of the "weaker sex." For the only admissible standard that survives the harsh measure of nature is strength—power and its trappings.

Of course the ethologists, if morally unsophisticated, are not vulgarians. They are clever enough to recognize the perils of uncurbed logic, and so have disguised their naturalism in what can be called prudential ethics—"if-then" reasoning that relegates moral questions to ifs we tend to take for granted while focusing on consequences in the more accessible realm of then. The ifs appear as givens, leaving only the thens to be debated, all in the comfortable setting of factual description and logical entailment. The entire enterprise aims at giving what are really only descriptive propositions a moral aura that permits them to pass as ethical. Thus, while to say "if you want to take the *best* way down town, then you *ought* to take the A train" has normative overtones and an imperative mien, it is in fact a disguised indicative with purely descriptive content, viz.: "A trains make the trip down town more efficiently than other trains, or alternative modes of transport." The real moral question, whether one *ought* to go down town, is lost by being subsumed as a given in a mode of discourse that stresses consequences.

Naturalists use this device with particular effect. Lionel Tiger, for example, never asserts that male bonding is good per se. He claims only that it is natural—a given—and that *if* men, as bonding animals, "need some haunts and/or occasions which exclude females," *then* society ought to provide them. George Gilder adopts the same prudential mode: *If* women wish to save civilization as it is defined by their "long-term perspectives," *then* they ought to avoid undermining "civilized male identity" by abdicating their traditional wifely and maternal roles in the name of liberation. The argument is relative not absolute, yet somehow is made to seem more rather than less urgent because of its appeal to givens that appear so inexorable.

The contingent "if " is, however, a treacherous conditional, for it conceals the only true moral question: within the necessary givens that condition us and between the competing natural desires that pull at us, how *ought* we to behave? what *ought* we to want? to which ideals *ought* we to aspire? We may want to go uptown not downtown, or believe we ought to go uptown even though we want to go downtown, in which case we ought *not* to take the A train. It is perfectly possible, to take a more pertinent issue, to accept that Gilder is correct in his *description* of civilization as a form of repression, yet to reverse his evaluative *judgement* and argue that animal expression is the greatest good and that, therefore, we ought to aim consciously at desocialization rather than socialization, barbarism rather than civilization and sexual expression rather than sexual repression (as Reichians and certain neo-Freudians actually do argue). By the same token, even if we entertain the proposition that sexual differentiation really does entail sexual inequality, (an argument whose refutation is the chief aim of this book), it is no less proper to demand the elimination of sexual differentiation (as some liberationists do) than to recommend the permanent deferral of equality (as naturalists do). In sum, we cannot evaluate the "ifs" without reference to moral standards that cannot themselves be derived from if-then reasoning. Nature cannot provide the norms by which nature is to be judged. It can tell us where we have been and where at a given moment we seem to be heading. It cannot tell us where we ought to be going, or whether the direction in which it heads us is the right direction. The ethologists tell us a great deal about ourselves as animals. But they tell us nothing about ourselves as humans. The naturalists write informative (if conflicting) accounts of our sexual origins. But the pages on which an account of our moral ends is to be inscribed remain blank. Natural ink will not take. The future awaits Will.

Steven Goldberg writes in the last chapter of *The Inevitability of Patriarchy*: "at the bottom of it all, man's job is to protect women and woman's is to protect her infant; in nature all else is luxury." Not quite. In nature, *all* except survival is luxury. The polity is luxury, language is luxury, morality is luxury, choice is luxury, equality is luxury, freedom is luxury. They are luxuries for which the species has fought these last ten thousand years, luxuries that have transformed childbearing female animals and plow-pushing male animals into women and men, luxuries that in a gradual conquest of nature's inefficiencies have made human beings out of beasts, luxuries that have endowed human will with the power to create human destiny.

It is a sad consequence of the war for and against nature, that civilization has been assailed by both sides —a luxurious facade to the naturalist, a trap to the liberationist. If civilization is taken as the sturdy trunk linking the roots of our animal past to the highest branches of our human future, then the naturalist appears as a displaced grub trying to burrow its way down from trembling branches into the safety of buried roots, while the liberationist seems a grounded swallow beating its wings against a labyrinth of roots keeping it from its perch next to paradise. Grub and swallow alike are oblivious to the trunk that is their common battlefield. They share the the deadly premise that roots and leaves have no common sap, and are thus indifferent to a withering of the trunk that will imperil roots and leaves alike. Their war is the war between nature and liberation, the war that presupposes, in Goldberg's didactic subtitle, that "the biological difference between men and women always produces male domination." *Always*, says the naturalist; so stop tampering with nature. *Always*, concurs the liberationist; so abolish nature, away with sexual differentiation. And so the warriors leave the rest of us with a terrible choice, an impossible choice: natural slavery or liberated androgyny, a natural, apolitical, inequitable heterosexuality that buys species survival with permanent injustice, or an unnatural, apolitical, equitable unisexuality that purchases personhood at the price of sexuality. Tied together by nature but alienated from ourselves, or emancipated from nature but alienated from each other.

An impossible choice, indeed; a choice whose distastefulness led me into the book and now propels me to the crucial stage of the analysis: an attempt to extricate the issues from the war for and against nature, and provide an alternative perspective for their resolution. The problem is clear enough. Unless a way can be found to make sexual differentiation compatible with equality and freedom, we will be doomed to the arid choices offered us by the warriors. We will face the awful decision whether to abandon our sexuality or abdicate forever the ideals of justice and freedom.

4

*Nature and Liberation
at Peace*

GERMAINE GREER HAS DRAMATIZED the contemporary plight of women with the epithet Female Eunuch. But the alternative for many liberationists seems to be the Human Eunuch—in place of the despotism of sex, an equitable neuterdom. Norman Mailer no doubt intends to pay an ironic compliment to his own thralldom with the title Prisoner of Sex, but to Carolyn G. Heilbrun *(Towards a Recognition of Androdgyny)* the reality is beyond irony: for her, we are all hapless captives of "the prison of gender" who can be saved from "self-brutalization" and "self-destruction" only by androgynous personhood.

In the ideal of androgyny, the fifth claim of the liberationists (left pending at the end of the second section) converges with the major premise of naturalism: that femininity and equality are intrinsically incompatible and that the suborning of sexuality is too high a price to pay for freedom. "Nature or Liberation!" becomes the common war cry of naturalists and liberationists alike, and the war rages on towards a resolution which, both sides allow, must issue either in natural slavery or in contrived androgyny.

More than one hundred years ago, in *The Subjection of Women*, John Stuart Mill wrote: "The moral regeneration of mankind will only really commence, when the most fundamental of the social relations is placed under the rule of equal justice, and when human beings learn to cultivate their strongest sympathy with an equal in rights and cultivation." Naturalists think this neither possible nor desirable; feminists believe it obligatory but deem it possible only with the attenuation of that "strongest sympathy" that, in tying the sexes together, has bound them to nature's common mastery.

The dilemma, as it issues from this implacable antagonism, is compounded by the fact that the natural condition assailed by feminism and defended by naturalism has long since been compromised by the artifices of our civilization. Nature is no longer master (the lesson of history), and personhood no longer merely a noble or dangerous aspiration, but a concrete reality in the eyes of the law, before which sexual differences are mostly inadmissable; the Equal Rights Amendment will give this reality constitutional status. Consequently, naturalists cannot really maintain their image as defenders of an adequate status quo, but appear as reactionary advocates of a biological childhood out of which the species has long since grown. At the same time, feminists trumpeting the remote virtues of liberation as a distant prospect, and doing battle on its behalf, fail to note certain of its virtues and many more of its vices are already upon us. Uprootedness, alienation and normlessness attest to the rise of free consciousness in the face of waning naturalism; they are pathologies that, as Midge Dechter argues in what is the most valid phase of her study, require something more than the cry for still more abstract liberty if they are to be treated.

In a way, our dilemma is that of the adolescent rebelling against natural parents whose authority has already passed in the name of an independence too unrooted, too abstract, too artificial, yet to be meaningful. The naturalist prefers the comforting heteronomy of parental authority to the burdens of liberation and so urges upon society a regressive return to infantilism where Father and Mother Nature will guide our lives with the sure strings of heterosexuality. Liberationists enjoy the prospect of independence and self-definition, but are bogged down in the deracinated irresponsibility of rebellion for its own sake, mindless of the need to invest newly autonomous identities with values and purposes drawn from the formative riches of early identity, despite its former heteronomy. It is not an easy situation, even for those who wish to keep growing towards full maturity.

To exercise autonomy apparently requires that all the norms and meanings associated with parental authority be decisively rejected; yet that leaves autonomy an empty form which, unless its choices can reconstruct meaning, becomes more self-alienating than self-liberating, more inimical to than supportive of self-realization. The liberation that facilitates the realization of self too often endangers the self to be realized. At the level of our biological identities, all of our interpersonal relations are invested with vital meanings by sexuality and its residues; yet these meanings too often seem to divest women (and men) of the qualities requisite to personhood, thus impeding justice and obstructing the path to personal liberation and self-realization. In a woman, maternity and personhood, the one mediated by nature, the other created by the autonomous will, are thus set at odds, giving to woman's condition a perilously schizophrenic character. If gender is truly a prison that, in making us women and men, deprives us of our common personhood, then we are doomed to be eternal prisoners of sex or to be emancipated Eunuchs with souls too sexless to be determinate, to be anything at all except free.

This bemusing dilemma is, however, itself the product of the melancholy war I have been condemning from the earliest pages of this book. It rests on the unacceptable premise that sexuality and equality, nature and freedom, roots and autonomy, are perpetual antagonists—inherently antithetical to one another in the abstract, and incompatible in the concrete psychological settings where they can be found polarizing everyday life. Be a mother or be a person, be a wife or be free: there is no middle, no third, no alternative way.

However, I hope I have shown that the premise of incompatibility—the belief that sexual differentation entails inequality—rests on a serious error. My intention is this section is to detail the consequences of this error and thereby point the way to terms of reconciliation that will put an end to the war over nature. Peace will liberate feminism from its crippling antinomies and open the way to a more vital struggle to reconstruct the polity in ways that serve both our sexuality and our human aspirations.

The error of thinking that sexual differences cause bigotry or render inequities of treatment inevitable has its source in a confusion about the character of equality as a social and political norm. To speak of equality is to prescribe certain modes of treating women and men, not to describe their comparative identities. It pertains to opportunities, not capacities. Indeed, it is the aim of egalitarianism to assure that beings who may well possess differing qualities and incommensurate capacities will nonetheless receive the same opportunities and the same impartial treatment at the hands of laws, institutions and their fellow beings. John Stuart Mill, in championing sexual egalitarianism, nevertheless was quite clear that "mere unlikeness, when it only means differences of good qualities, may be more a benefit in the way of mutual improvement, than a drawback from comfort." Differences, per se, enrich and guarantee a nourishing diversity. They are at the core of sexuality's pleasures for women and men. Mill's prophetic assault on sexual discrimination could comfortably include a nostalgic tribute to chivalry, an institution which Mill understood as complimenting sexual differences without compromising sexual equality. Its refusal to dichotomize sexuality and equality make the relevant passage worth citing at some length:

Though the practice of chivalry fell even more sadly short of its theoretic standard than practice generally falls be-

low theory, it remains one of the most precious monu-
ments of the moral history of our race; as a remarkable
instance of a concerted and organized attempt by a most
disorganized and distracted society, to raise up and carry
into practice a moral ideal greatly in advance of its social
condition and institutions; so much so as to have been
completely frustrated in the main object, yet never en-
tirely inefficacious, and which has left a most sensible, and
for the most part a highly valuable impress on the ideas
and feelings of all subsequent times.

A liberated woman, Mill would seem to argue, can take
untroubled pleasure in the complimentary rituals by
which men open doors before them—as long as the doors
are held open, not shut, and lead into polling booths and
executive suites as well as into kitchens and nurseries.
The chivalrous politenesses made possible by heterosexuality are more than just harmless: they are essential to
a rewarding and civilized interdependence.

Not that differences cannot often be abused as a ra-
tionale for bias. Whenever people are different from one
another there is a potential for antipathy and prejudice.
Only a race of unisexual robots pressed from a single
mold would be immune to bigotry. To be a necessary
condition of bias is not, however, to be a sufficient condition. Bias is an attitude toward differences that is linked
with the problem of autonomy. When comparative differences that constitute the attributes of an identity are
associated with a caricatured "natural" stereotype imposed from the outside by antagonists, or inflicted by the
decree of a nature we do not choose for ourselves, the

we do not choose for ourselves, the result of differentiation is prejudice and self-hatred, and the likely political
outcome, discrimination. But when the same attributes,
whether natural or acquired, are associated with an autonomously chosen archetype that serves as a model for
positive self-realization, the result can only be enriching
diversity and enhanced self-pride.

Stereotypes are intrinsically pejorative and serve to
alienate people from themselves; archetypes are con-
structive idealizations that play a necessary and creative
role in achieving an integral, mature identity.
Stereotypical blackness, for example, caricatures certain
"natural" traits in pejorative terms (singin' an' dancin',
the shuffle, Colored People's Time), alienating blacks
from possible ingredients of a cultural identity and driving them into self-annihilating emulation of alien archetypes. The failure of integration was due in part to
its tendency to compel a rejection of blackness in favor
of whiteness in the struggle for equality. More recently,
blacks have come to reject the stereotypical abuse of their
racial features and cultural heritage and to accept blackness as a kind of archetypical model for collective and
individual identity. Characteristics demeaned by mock-
ing racists become positive when freely ackno ledged
and celebrated by approving blacks: to have rhythm
becomes hip, C.P.T. means screw the uptight, clock-
bound ofay, and blackness becomes a polished ebony
mirror of "soul." And what is soul here but a keyword
for an archetype? Black *is* beautiful . . . as an archetype;
it is ugly only in the stereotypes of bigots.

Although the plight of blacks and of women is strik-

ingly different—sexuality having deeper biological roots
and more pervasive cultural impact than race, blackness
being far more subject to oppression than femininity—
femininity is in this particular sense no different than
blackness. As a stereotype imposed by sexist men, a
manipulative society or by women whom (as Greer
provocatively observes) society has turned into maso-
chists, womanliness is synonymous with inadequacy,
deficiency, inferiority—weak passivity that invites
abuse, corrupt genitalia that must be gingerly deodo-
rized, little minds that require continuous guidance.
Wallace Reyburn, in his pathetic tract *The Inferior Sex*,
thus organizes his woman-hating petulance around
stereotypes like vanity, crudity and "catty-bitchy-
viciousness," allowing at the same time that calling
women bitches insults dogs; (this passes for high wit
with Reyburn, since among the half-witted low looks
high). Bigots can be dismissed, but too many women in
quest of liberation have accepted this same stereotype,
and spend their energies struggling to exorcise as de-
monic, natural facets of their identities that could be
regarded as angels. Recall Juliet Mitchell's portrait of
women as "small-minded, pettily jealous, irrationally
emotional, randomly violent, dependent, competitively
selfish and conservative." Suppose she had written
"down to earth, monogamous, close to their feelings,
unrepressed, loving, self-approving and conservation-
ist"? How radically a change in tone alters the portrait,
though the characteristics depicted are much the same.

It is precisely this acquiescence in the face of abusive
stereotypes that compels feminists to antithesize

femininity and equality and hence suppose that the achievement of dignity demands the annihilation of nature, that liberation calls for the uprooting of identity from the rich humus of sexuality. Compared to black liberationists, women liberationists appear trapped in the integrationist phase of their rebellion, permitting hostile stereotypes to rob them of archetypes, allowing the name-callers to steal from them their name. Yet, if they would but see it, there is power as well as comfort in the slogan Woman is Beautiful (Black is Beautiful)— a power that repels hostile stereotypes by embracing as ideals the characteristics stereotypes assay to belittle.

A satisfactory archetype has little to do with the fictional goddess with which the male imagination complements its odious "bitch" stereotype, and is certainly not to be discovered in the literary supplications of a swooning Norman Mailer or in the pedestaled compliments of a genuflecting Ashley Montagu. It can only arise out of a woman's voluntary acquiescence in and modification of a nature she chooses for herself; it gains its force from her willed adoption of instinctive pressures for feminine modes of self-expression. The free woman might thus conceive of herself as (for example) receptive, enduring, intuitive, maternal and tender, and might then construct from these "natural" attributes an archetype which would serve as a model of self-realization, much as the rebellious Catholic might after a period of reasoned doubt in the wilderness reassume his religion with the conviction of rational belief. Yet in constructing her archetype, she could perfectly well reject the stereotypical counterparts, and refuse to behave or

be treated as a passive victim (the stereotypical equivalent of receptivity), a plodding mule (endurance), an irra-
tional hysteric (intuition), a narrow-minded cow (maternity), or a surrogate pillow (tenderness).

Archetypes do not reflect weaknesses, they underscore
strengths; they are not imposed caricatures but chosen
ideals—compatible, to be sure, with natural proclivities,
but distinguished from them by the critical intervention
of will in their impact on character. For a woman to say
she is intuitive is not then to say she cannot be rigorously
analytical or acutely logical; it is only to say she is also,
and perhaps especially, intuitive—intuition being itself
a mode of reasoning. Elizabeth Gould Davis, arguing in
a utopian key towards the end of *The First Sex*, sustains
her belief that "woman's contribution to civilization is
greater than man's" by an appeal to woman's "spiritual
force," her "mental and spiritual gifts." Intuition, what
she calls the power to "see the unseen," is thus conse-
crated as a defining strength rather than rejected as a
villainous frailty.

By the same token, for a woman to say she is receptive
does not imply she is abnormally vulnerable or peculiarly passive; it is to say her potency manifests itself with
special conviction in the capacity to contain and envelop
both physically and emotionally. For a woman to say she
is tender does not require that she countenance abuse or
admit weakness; tenderness is a strength, an assertive
capacity to give love unjudgmentally and non-contractu-
ally. In the provocative *New York Times* article "Up from
the Kitchen Floor," (March 4, 1973) summing up her
decade of struggle, Betty Friedan wrote with moving

simplicity: "I would have lost my feeling for the woman's movement if I had not been able, finally, to admit tenderness." To fight, conscious of tenderness, is still to fight: but it is to fight without forgetting where the struggle began, and where if successful, it will end.

Whatever the psychology of its genesis, lesbianism can even be regarded as a separatist attempt to explore the meaning of feminine archetypes—to acquire dignity and status for attributes too often damaged on the battle-ground of heterosexuality. Simone de Beauvoir observed long ago in *The Second Sex* that the "refusal to make herself the object is not always what turns woman to homosexuality; most lesbians, on the contrary, seek to cultivate the treasures of their femininity." Ingrid Bengis *(Combat in the Erogenous Zone)* cites both this passage and the one below from Sylvia Plath's *The Bell Jar* in trying to convey the psychic topography of lesbianism:

> "What does a woman see in a woman that she can't see in a man?" Doctor Nolan paused. Then she said, "Tenderness."

Although certain lesbian liberationists march under androgynous banners, androgyny's true soldiers are permitted neither tenderness nor any of the other insignia issued by the enemy. Not even lesbianism can survive neuterdom's uniformities.

Masculine archetypes can potentially also be salutory, albeit, like femininity, they tend to be more often abused as stereotypes than used as models for mature self-realization. Archetypically, masculinity focuses on attributes such as assertiveness and the proclivity for analytic dissection, attributes which do not, however, require us to tolerate their stereotypical counterparts (machismo and aggressiveness for assertiveness, insensitivity and partial vision for analyticity). Both receptivity (the vagina construed as trap) and assertiveness (the penis construed as bludgeon) can be weapons in abusive hands; neither is necessarily so. When we permit stereotypes to define archetypes, when Yang and Yin are reduced to bully and victim, we succeed only in defining the best in men and women in terms of the worst.

Nor do archetypes impose limits on types of activity or modes of behavior. Beyond the obviously sexual ones, there are no peculiarly womanly or manly activities. Literary and artistic creation, science, business and even war are human activities for which women and men are, as humans, by definition capable. There is, however, a womanly way and a manly way of carrying on each of these activities—not better, not worse, simply different. Germans and Italians eat differently, Japanese and Irish greet differently, and Pakistani and Americans pray differently. But they all feed themselves, they all follow rituals of encounter, they all seek communion with a deity. Women police officers patrol the streets, make arrests, interrogate suspects and so forth, but each of these activities is mediated by the feminine qualities they bring to the position. Those qualities may be particularly suitable in some situations (household squabbles, rape) and less suitable in others (calming an enraged, drunken, cuckolded misogynist bent on revenge), but they are never disqualifications per se. The cry of androgyny is too often a disguise for the attempt to turn women into men in order to "qualify" them for existence in a man's world. This deceit only forfeits victory to the sexists, for it permits the confounding of style and capacity to persist, while requiring of women who would enter the active world the sacrifice of their feminine identities.

Liberationists lend the credibility of a struggle for freedom to these confusions when they insist that the only security against abuse by stereotype is the abolition of archetype. Get rid of the concept "Woman" and there can never again be chicks, or skirts or dolls. If you refuse to conceive of yourself as a woman, you never need risk being called a cunt. The same goes for men: abjure manhood and you will never be a prick. But at what price. And how unnecessarily costly. Autonomously chosen ideals are not heteronomous caricatures, even if, as is inevitable in the development of human personality, ideals are derived in part from genetic, biological and naturally acquired cultural characteristics. To make this mistake is to replicate the errors of polarizing nature and freedom. If the purpose of human liberation is the realization of the full human self of each individual woman and man, archetypes can be regarded as crucial allies— foundations of growth, the substance by which free identities are delimited, the crucial link between our unchosen natural heritage and the chosen attributes of our willed destinies. Identities are not chosen in vacuo, like items in an alien cafeteria. The arbitrary construction of a new self without regard to personal history, roots, or needs has more in common with schizophrenia than with liberation. Somehow, freedom has come to mean the shucking not merely of clothes, but of skin as well— a process of spiritual evisceration in which nature's organs are spilled out and nature's blood drained away to be replaced by motors and formaldehyde. The stuffed automaton who results is presumably liberated from the constraints of its previous nature.

Nancy Walker, an enterprising spiritual taxidermist, recently tried quite literally to "swap lives" with another rather less enthusiastic young woman; the resulting second-best seller (*The Life Swap*) catches the absurdist tone of arbitrary self-definition perfectly. Nancy Walker asks winningly:

> If it isn't our right and our gravest obligation to invent ourselves, reinvent ourselves, can we be said to exist at all? To be a single personality, fixed and final, would be to render ourselves unable to love all those we might love, serve everything we consider worthy, honor the magnificent contradictoriness of life . . .

Invent ourselves? As if identity could be constructed from the pieces of an Erector Set? Never be fixed or final? Oh yes, if only the endless possibilities, the illusory infinities of adolescence could last forever. Be saddled with only one personality? Better, a life of serial schizophrenia, a permanent quest for impermanence. Ingrid Bengis, of course, knows better. She is less interested in occupying the soul of a roommate than in living with herself. Her candor is a simple warning:

In the process of attempting to become "separate individuals" many of us have had to anesthetize ourselves to needs that are nonetheless real and deep. We have rationalized our desires for love and affection, permanence and stability, equating those desires with a capitulation to unresolved weaknesses in ourselves.

The result, Bengis concludes, is that the freedom in the name of which needs are slighted "all too often seems hollow when it is achieved." Hollow, I would offer, because it is not freedom at all, only the skeleton of freedom—empty choice, pointless options, none of which have meaning in a deracinated world where the only clues to identity have been declared contraband because they are known to the enemy. How can a woman be expected to find sustenance in a cafeteria of values and meanings where the menu scrupulously offers everything in creation except the nourishment of her own past? Old identities cannot simply be discarded because they are weighed down with childhood fears, adolescent neuroses and the stereotypical abuses of enemies of growth; hidden in fears and neuroses and stereotypes are seeds of growth, the promise of adult possibilities. Just as in the authoritarian rituals and blind fears of the awestruck altar boy is hidden a potential Christian capable of autonomous conviction and authentic belief.

Sometimes the quest for liberation from natural identity is justified by an appeal to the "quintessential human" that resides in each woman and man, and may be hidden, repressed, even imprisoned by womanhood or

manhood. But human personhood is a vital legal fiction
that secures social and political equality of treatment and
opportunity, not, as I have argued, a psychological cate-
gory or a growth ideal. The demands made upon us by
our humanity—communication, justice, equity, fairness
—do not alter the fact that *human* beings do not exist.
Not in isolation, in the abstract, pristinely. Humanity
manifests itself in persons who are specifiable only by
virtue of additional characteristics. We are Moslem or
Christian humans, plumber or farmer humans, Chinese
or American humans, philosopher or fool humans,
women or men humans. But never simply human humans.

Humanity can be institutionalized as a moral ideal,
but not realized as a personality archetype. To think
otherwise is to subscribe to what I call the onion-peeling
fallacy, which assumes that the truly human being "un-
derlying" the layers and layers of education, socialization, role-identification, politicization, indoctrination
and acculturation in which society and culture have
wrapped us will be discovered only when we pursue a
ruthless strategy of peeling. To get to the human being
in a woman requires peeling away femininity, and sexuality and biology itself if necessary, to get to the naked
core. What the onion-peeling fallacy suggests, however,
is that when all of the multiple layers and secondary
accretions are stripped away in the quest for the essential
core, the onion itself may disappear. Because, having no
pith, the onion quite literally *is* its multiple layers; and
the "inside" layers are no more definitive of its identity
than the "outside" layers. If humans are to be peeled,

aggressive peelers may discover that in denuding them of sexual and other natural and social attributes, they denude them of human essence altogether. Strip away masculinity and femininity from men and women and you get not humans but neuter things with no discernible identity at all. Women are not human beings clothed in a removable mantle of femininity, they are woman-human-beings whose humanity is expressed in and through (among many other attributes) their womanhood.

The great French conservative of the early nineteenth century, Joseph deMaistre, once wrote with feigned puzzlement: "I have seen in my time Frenchmen, ⁱ⁺alians and Russians; I even know, thanks to Montesquieu, that one may be a Persian; but as for *man*, I declare that I have never met him in my life; if he exists, it is without my knowledge." As for myself: I have seen men, and I have seen women; but human beings? I have never met one in my life. They do exist, in a sense. They can be found in the law courts where due process is being observed, in constitutions where rights are guaranteed without respect to race, creed, religion and (if the Equal Rights Amendment is finally enacted) sex, and in codes of ethics that prescribe duties and justify obligations. But you cannot meet them, or emulate them or make them the object of self-realization. Does anyone really want to grow up to be a human? Be treated as one, yes. But simply *be* one? And what would one be? A fiction? An abstraction? Shulamith Firestone may actually aspire to such an end: she wants to rid us not only of the "joyless labor" of the factory, but also of the "joyless labor" of the childbed. In her awesome human utopia, the pain of birth and the labor of creation are not to be distinguished from the pain of death and the labor of self-destruction. But such a world cannot exist.

The androgynous ideal, when it is not merely femininity masquerading as Everyman—Amazons in the garb of Everyhuman—is psychologically vacant, developmentally meaningless. The just aim of feminism is the liberation of women from abuse; the liberation of women from womanhood serves that goal only as suicide serves the mitigation of suffering. The goal of personal self-realization is the fulfillment of the potential of women and men as members of the human polity; an abstract emancipation from natural identity that leaves individuals adrift with free-floating, transient characters guaranteed to be as meaningless as they are autonomous serves self-realization not at all. To choose meaningfully; to invest freedom with significance; to root ideals in reality while transforming reality with ideals; and to accommodate the guiding dictates of a no longer omnipotent nature with the moral standards of an increasingly potent autonomy: these are the real tasks of liberation.

Humanness is the leading principle, but not the humanness of peeled onions or the humanness of abstract personhood. For our humanity is in the layers digging peelers would strip away. Naturalists and liberationists have in common a desire to get to the pith of being, hoping to discover there some animal essence or transessential spirit—some grunting mammalian biped instinctively ejecting more of its kind into a world ruled by death, or a silent deity contemplating deathless eternity in solitary beatitude. Such beings may encircle us in the shadows beyond the communal fire, troubling our sleep with solipsistic nightmares and tempting our individualism with smoky visions of an unattainable solitude—the born freedom of beasts and gods—but they do not define us as we huddle together around the flames. For we are defined as human by our sociability, not our solitude, by the reluctant interdependence to which our insufficiencies condemn us, not by the futile pride of our individuality (which failed us before history ever began).

The human polity alone endows freedom with substance and invests with meaning lives forsaken by nature. The common agreements of the polity replace nature's laws with our own, substitute for nature's blind drives seeing motivations and conscious ideals. The struggle for identity is an ineluctably social struggle, the battle for self-realization winnable only in the framework of the polity. It is a commonplace of psychology that the self as a mature and integrated entity is defined by its interaction with other selves, by obligations and commitments, by duties and responsibilities, by love and by need. It discovers itself in work made significant by the values and goals of the polity, in ceremonies that derive their power from rituals of the polity, in relationships endowed with stability and mutuality by the structures of the polity.

This is the more profound meaning of sexuality, which is only secondarily a function of hormones and orifices, of nature's formula for survival. It is primarily a reflection of the humanizing offices of civilization: of

society's division of labor, of art's pursuit of a beauty that
will not suffer uniformity, of custom's predilection for
ritual, of the polity's concern for generations already
dead and generations yet to be born. The realization of
the human potential is a mutualist enterprise for which
women and men, as complementary beings who need
each other to be complete, are particularly well suited.
When they isolate themselves and try to extract from
their identities an individuated, autonomous core, they
only diminish their humanity. As Philip Slater, never
less than wise, remarks in his most recent book *Earthwalk*, "The notion that people begin as separate individuals, who then march out and connect themselves
with others, is one of the most dazzling bits of self-
mystification in the history of the species." Dazzling and
powerful; for it has become the philosophy of western
individualism, the ideology of a great deal of specious
psychology, and the favorite rationalization of naturalists and liberationists in their mutually misanthropic
wars.

The terms of peace then, that can bring tranquility to
the restless spirits on both sides of the trenches, dictate
an acknowledgment of mutualism, a recognition of the
polity's challenge to apolitical individualism. These
terms offer standards for human growth that are relevant to our natural needs, yet still voluntary and consensual. They offer a freedom that is lawful without being
tyrannical, liberating without being alienating; for it is,
as John Stuart Mill depicted it, "the liberty of each to
govern his conduct by his own feelings of duty, and by
such laws and social restraints as his own conscience can

subscribe to." In this, they offer us identities that are our own, because we choose them, but each other's as well, because they are grounded in our mutual relations and modeled after archetypes that define at once our diversity and our interdependence. They offer, too, standards for choice that are substantive without being heteronomous, consensual without being arbitrary, and meaningful without being absolute.

The terms of peace are not yet a program for liberation, but in stipulating its context, they make a program possible. Once the war over nature is ended, the quest for liberation can begin. Once feminism is liberated from the narrow perspectives that put it at odds with the femininity its name ennobles, it can begin its true struggle: to rescue the polity in which our humanity resides from its myriad enemies, and thereby to rescue women from the precarious perch somewhere between animality and divinity where their search for liberation has left them.

5

Liberating Feminism—
A Program

THE APPEAL TO THE HUMAN POLITY CONJURES, I trust, a rich image of our interdependence and our mutualistic diversity as a species *sui generis*. Yet the polity is an abstraction that may seem to divert attention from the vital programmatic reforms current conditions demand. In fact, I want to contend, a preoccupation with the larger question of the healthy polity enjoins a great deal in the way of practical reform, and suggests changes that go well beyond the reformist, often inadvertently establishmentarian action plans of feminist organizations like the National Organization of Women, or the charged but vague rhetoric of more extreme elements in the movement. For the first order of business for feminists withdrawing from the war on nature is the reconstruction of the polity as a nourishing environment for liberation. The defining condition of liberty, when no longer at odds with nature, is the polity. The defining condition of the free woman who no longer feels impelled to surrender her sexuality to achieve her self-liberation is the free polity. This suggests a monumental program of change. It is not simply that the American polity is not free; it is not in any relevent sense a polity at all, if by polity we are to understand a community of free citizens who derive from their mutual relations the primary values and meanings of their existence as human beings.

The market and the machine have together conspired to reduce free polities to stagnant bureaucracies that use and control the race that created them. Capitalism and technology, each a tool of our gradual subjugation of nature, make a mockery of our emancipation by subduing and subjugating us in turn. There is hardly a pathology that afflicts us as children of modernity that cannot be traced to darker facets of the competitive systems and scientific discoveries whose contributions have permitted us progress. Uniformity, technocratism, irresponsibility, hedonism, alienation, bureaucratism, anomie, narcissism, infantalism, acquisitiveness and amoralism—the in many cases rewarding diseases of the body, and the almost always debilitating diseases of the spirit —these have been the price exacted by our unlimited growth, our unprecedented affluence, our unrelenting progress. The cost has been particularly high to the polity.

The *agora*, once the meeting place of citizens pursuing public purposes, is now a market place for products— citizens too having become products. Human relations and social relations are now market relations that make of women and men, consumers and producers—who themselves are but commodities. Competition overtakes cooperation, acquisitiveness sinks generosity, and self-interest is turned from an efficient operating principle into a society-wide ideal. Alienated from the social bodies (including the family) that might have endowed their ends with social purposes, and cut off from the sense of communality that might have made mutualism seem worthwhile, women and men are thrown back on venal hedonism and material self-interest—endowments which, far from being satisfying, only complete the circle of alienation by alienating women and men from their last resource: themselves. The competitive, atomistic atmosphere engendered by market relations can only fragment social intercourse and paralyze the polity. Ideas like fraternity that are critical to the communal life of polities—Wilson Carey McWilliams' *The Idea of Fraternity in America* attests powerfully to its indispensability —are left to expire, or hastened to their demise by campaigns impeaching their Americanism, or their relevance, or their liberality.

The machine, no less potent in our emancipation from nature's inefficiencies than the market, has been no less injurious to the idea of polity. Its potency is in the instrumentalism that defines its purposes: transferred to human relations, instrumentalism promotes an interpersonal usury that polities cannot survive. When we use one another as means to self-interested ends, when the machine interposes itself between our creative labor power and the products it turns out, when as a powerfully suggestive metaphor it turns our human world into a cosmos of force vectors and predetermined causal interactions, the dark side of the machine creeps into the daylight—a shadow across its indisputable contribution to our long-term rise to civilized personhood.

Both the market and the machine are then two-edged swords—one blade cutting the bonds of our natural thralldom, the other, at the very moment we become sensible to our liberation, cutting the bonds of our political mutuality and civilizing communality and plunging us into a new and more frightening bondage. You are free, the market proclaims . . . and impotent. For *it* shall now step into nature's shoes, vacated by the conquest of scarcity. You are liberated, cries the machine . . . and alone. For men serve the machines that serve them, and lose sight of their fellow beings working—or, thanks to the machine, playing—by their sides.

I do not mean to commence a new book, however. The perils of markets and machines have been extensively remarked upon with the conscientiousness their significance deserves by Philip Slater, Theodore Roszak, John Kenneth Galbraith, C. Wright Mills, C. P. Snow, Jacques Ellul and the rest of that remarkable tribe of seers who by their criticism expose how frail our society has become, and by their insight manage nonetheless to shore it up. Nor is it quite fair to say to women trying to achieve incremental changes in their status and piecemeal improvements in their practical condition that they ought instead to be busy with the larger struggle to reconstruct the polity. The larger struggle is also more remote, less probable, a distant rumble out of earshot when voices close by are cursing, "Stay home, bitch!" If incremental reforms must be deferred while quantum leap revolutions are undertaken, if better wages must await the elimination of corporate capitalism and better attitudes the elimination of the market mentality, liberation may be centuries in coming. Can the housewife contemplating adultery, or suicide or the abandonment of her family afford to go to war with capitalism? Can the frustrated college graduate be asked to remake the world so that her entry into it will be humanizing rather than alienating?

Probably not. And my purpose in reciting the catalog of our society's deficiencies as they affect the decline of the polity is not to transform the woman's movement into a general strike, or a socialist rebellion or a permanent revolution. Not exactly. On the other hand, it *is* my intent to persuade liberationists that there will be no freedom without a reconstructed polity, that meaningful self-realization for women and for men entails the recreation of mutualism. This does not mean that liberation must be subsumed to the idea of polity; it does mean that the idea of polity must be incorporated in liberation. The woman's movement cannot eradicate the alienating anomie of self-interested individualism in the society at large, but it can pursue self-conscious, responsible mutualism in its own programs. The action program of woman's rights need not reconstruct the polity, but but it had better understand the forces that destroy it. It cannot be responsible for the multiple transgressions of modernity against humankind, but it must be certain its own "reforms" do not aggravate those transgressions still more. Each of the "crises" that we seem to stumble into year after year are predictable episodes in the history of materialistic individualism's human self-

alienation, predictable stages in the processes of market
and machine through which our polities have been un-
dermined and our mutual interdependence ruptured.

The energy crisis testifies to the blindness of narcissistic consumerism and mindless acquisition, the crisis of
marriage to the pubescent willfulness of arbitrary independence and the erosion of commitment as a prerequisite of human (if not carnal) relations, the racial crisis to
the potency of stereotypes run wild, the monetary crisis
to the venality of the international market, the crisis in
faith (the so-called Death of God) to the impotence of
rational emancipation from nature when it is unin-
formed by rooted beliefs, and the Watergate crisis to the
profound decline of a polity that was in trouble long
before that now deposed band of small-minded, unpatri-
otic careerists tried to feed the remains of the constitution to their ubiquitous shredders. The woman's movement, preoccupied with the crisis of women and the
crisis of the family, cannot play the universal healer. But
it must recognize the larger puzzle of which its preoccu-
pations are but pieces.

What is required is not the abandonment of piecemeal
programs but their reorientation; not a practical change
in reform efforts but a change in attitude about the aims
of reform—and the inevitable costs that have to be paid
but must not be forgotten. Consciousness-raising has
been a cliché of various "human liberation" programs,
but in many cases their real impact has been to repress
the kinds of consciousness demanded by our condition:
political consciousness, historical consciousness—a consciousness that is retrospective as well as introspective,

thou-conscious as well as I-conscious, cost-wary as
well as growth-greedy, polity-nourishing as well as ego-
feeding. A consciousness of our interdependence and of
the larger context of the polity will promote an ethos of
change that anticipates its own costs and remedies its
short-term defects. Programs informed by such an ethos
will regard men as allies, not enemies; they will see in
marriage a possible sanctuary for mutualism and a build-
ing block of just polities and will aim at their restoration
rather than their destruction; they will see children as
independent personalities who are also facets of our own
identity as they link us to the future and pay tribute to
our belief in the worthwhileness of living; they will generate and pursue archetypes rooted in need and in com-
formity with nature's strengths unafraid of the abusive
stereotypes to which ideals are always subject; they will
exploit the power of love and use the civilizing force of
myth to reinforce our institutions and gird our beliefs;
and such programs, finally, will never permit nature and
liberation to be set at odds, conscious that in the just
polity they can be at peace.

The liberation of feminism is not, then, itself a program. It is a mood, a tone, an orientation, an ethos—a
vital consciousness that can inform feminist programs
with a sensitivity to the environment in which changes
are going to take place, and the limitations that environment imposes on aspirations. It is not hard to imagine
how specific feminist programs might be modified, redi-
rected, or in many cases simply strengthened if their
reevaluation were to be informed by this expanded
awareness. Without trying to be exhaustive or particu-

larly programmatic, I can indicate the impact that consciousness of the sort I am urging might have on three
critical facets of our present dilemma: work, sex and
marriage. These remarks are exemplary rather than con-
clusive, for liberating feminism is a question of attitudes,
not programs.

A programmatic approach to the problems of women
wishing to work that was aware of the larger perspectives of the polity would be conscious of the economic
differences between working for self-expression and
working for survival, and work out priorities accordingly. It would avoid romanticizing work in the struggle
to give meaning to leisure, and would be wary of intensi-
fying the deadly competitive games of an acquisitive society by adding indiscriminately to the number of play-
ers. It would try not to pit work against children or
women's jobs against men's jobs in families that ought to
be seeking mutualist accommodation. The decision to
have children would entail several years of intensive parental involvement and an agreement by *both* parents to
compromise career involvements accordingly. It would
seek adequate child-care facilities for women and men
who must work but encourage others to participate ac-
tively in early childhood education—its aim being the
strengthening rather than the fragmentation of families.

Certain radical reforms might issue from such an approach. For example, the need for both partners in a
marriage to both work and participate in the raising of
children would suggest that the labor market be restruc-
tured wherever possible, and at the cost of efficiency if
necessary, to accommodate part-time workers. The total-

istic careerism that, however trivial it appears in perspective, can consume the overly-zealous office-dweller or ambitious professional would thus be avoided, while both partners would have time to share their children and satisfy their needs for self-expression. The burdens of both work and leisure would be more equitably shared, while single families would not be extracting double incomes from an economy hardly able to provide one per family. The added leisure, for both women and men, might also make possible that extended involvement in local community and polity so vital to the long-term reconstruction of mutualism. There are few job categories where four-hour days or two-and-one-half-day weeks would be out of the question, and many where it could be an advantage (where concentration for short periods was important, or where good nature in the face of consumer pressure was essential). Even high level offices could profit from being split: Switzerland sustains a highly efficient seven-man executive in which the honorific Presidency rotates annually. But impracticability ought not in any case to be decisive: there is nothing very practical about democracy and freedom, and civilization itself seems a good deal less practical than barbarism. The only viable economic structure, in the long run, is the one that serves women and men and the polities in which they choose freely to live.

The programmatic approach to marriage that would be likely to issue from a liberated feminist movement would have as its chief end the restoration of its mutualism and the revitalization of its links to the free polity. This would suggest the attenuation of rigid stereotypical roles in favor of a sharing of tasks and activities that calls on both partners to perform in their own distinctively archetypical ways jobs that are presently allotted by stereotypical features of femininity and masculinity. But neither fixed schedules nor universal labor allotments would be dictated in recognition of the fact that couples will differ and needs of individuals will change over time. Men who enjoy cooking will at times be weary, women who shop enthusiastically may at times need solitude.

The point of marriage is precisely to accommodate over a period of years the mutual needs and aspirations of persons who will not always be able to give as much as they get. Children too will thus learn the frailties of adults and be initiated into the mysteries of responsibility. It is one of the stunning peculiarities of American home life that nothing is expected of children, who repay their parent's indifference (disguised as freedom) with a precocious rebelliousness that keeps them in adolescence for twenty or thirty anomic years. The allegedly nuclear family has in reality often been dyadic, excluding children with the same hostilities shown the world. Because marriage challenges the capacities even of the most stable adults, the approach urged here would advocate that marriage be made more difficult, and divorce less accessible. Neo-Victorian stereotypes that require marriage of sexual partners and children of cohabitation do not, as usually thought, promote marriage at the expense of youthful adventurism; they erode marriage by making it a prerequisite of simple pleasures and sexual learning that are far better served by limited partnerships than permanent communities (which is what good marriages create).

Commitments do take time as well as mature knowledge of self; bearing and raising children asks still more. We issue licenses to drive and warrants to kill and certificates of higher education to teach only after certain relevant standards are met. To drive a car, or be a soldier or receive an M.A. requires proven aptitudes and demonstrated skills. To bear children and care for them over sixteen or twenty years we require only the capacity to copulate. And we entrust ourselves to the love and care of one another at the wink of an eye or the stiffening of an organ. No wonder so many partners flee each other in horror when they realize the responsibilities they have assumed and the inadequacies they have brought to the task. Children cannot be truly loving partners—they are too busy finding themselves—let alone be parents to other children. Marriage is not a contract: it is a commitment that, regardless of rewards, must be honored. Women and men who married later would have time to explore the world, potential careers, and themselves. Yearning adulterers are often unspoiled bridegrooms; impatient, frustrated wives often B.A.s who graduated into wedlock.

Making divorce less feasible is prudent only if marriage is more viable. Once adults have made commitments, their primary purposes ought to revolve around honoring them, for only thus can they honor their own souls. Too often, the first approach of clouds sends spouses dodging for cover, and the first drops of rain are permitted to dissolve all bonds. Back they flee to the seeming shelter of a society that has long since been inundated by far more severe storms. New partnerships entered into with still more uncertainty fare no better, and are either terminated sooner or endured with a resolve that might easily have salvaged the earlier vows. I mean no Calvinist lessons on suffering punishment by these remonstrations, only that marriage more often expires for lack of will and commitment than for lack of compatibility or love. The spirit of liberated feminism could do much to sustain will and reinforce commitment.

An approach to sex, the third example I have elected to touch on, would be informed by much the same ethos. In place of all the manuals of technique and guides to orgasm (the good ones say as much anyway), would be offered this dictum: human sex is not a physical act, it is a myth—one of our race's most splendid myths, its least dispensable myth. Among animals sex is precisely a physical act; among humans it is a psychic and social act in a physical setting. Sexual relations thus mirror human relations unfailingly. Casual relations beget indifferent sex, novel relations beget adventurous sex, competitive relations beget imperious sex, fearful relations beget impotent sex, bored relations beget pleasureless sex, hostile relations beget aggressive sex, and frivolous relations beget meaningless sex; and at the deeper level, committed relations beget liberated sex, loving relations beget profound sex and permanent relations beget the transcendent sex of *willed* conception—a form of sex permitted only to the human imagination, a form that has been the foundation of our civilization and the rockbed of our polity. Marital relations, when marriage is a link in the mutualist superstructure constituting the polity, will be committed, loving and permanent and will bestow on partners riches that diversity and novelty cannot offer. There is room enough for sex of every sort in a diversified society, but marital sex like marital relations makes certain demands that are as necessary as they are (at times) burdensome.

Marriage cannot tolerate adultery—call it freedom, or open marriage, or mutual independence or what you will—but marriage will not stand for it by any name. That is the cost of our dependence, the price of our commitments, the sacrifice offered to trust. The cynics will scoff and the cosmopolitans will wink, but you will not find a woman who can love or trust completely a man who shares their common bed with others; or a man whose commitment will not be shaken by his wife's affair. Marriage is troubled enough in its present condition, and sacred enough in its ideal state to warrant a rule that weakness may often infringe but that principle will not breach: marital fidelity and sexual infidelity are incompatible. Even Masters and Johnson, in their new book with the predictable title *The Pleasure Bond*, admit as much. Feminists endorsing this approach will confront the double standard in sexual relations, then, not by encouraging increased promiscuity and adultery in women but by pressing for increased commitment and fidelity in men, hoping to create a climate in which both men and women will benefit more from a freely chosen monogamy than from the mandatory polygamy of our present times. Even Frederick Engels in his radical critique of capitalist sexism believed that the real equality of women would "result far more effectively in men becoming really monogamous than in women becoming polygamous."

Programs of reform will then, if they are informed by the ethos of liberated feminism, seek always to enrich, never to impoverish, in the name of emancipation. In treating, for example, the sexist abuse of titles they may prefer reintroducing the distinction between Master (for single men) and Mr. (for married) to reducing Mrs. and Miss to an impoverished Ms. At the same time a universal "M." could be adopted for use in all formal situations and relations where personhood rather than sexuality and marital status was at stake. It is not terribly important, but Ms. is a move towards the dreary uniformity and actuarial dehumanization that is suggested to me by the use of numbers.

In confronting the relationship between consumer capitalism and the family, programs will, moreover, seek to insulate the family from contractualization, alienation and other capitalist pathologies rather than aid capitalism in its ongoing assault on marriage. Understanding that the market mentality has produced corrupt marital partnerships, they will use the revival of familial mutualism as a weapon against an interest-infected society. They will acknowledge the power of complex myths in lending meaning to life, and oppose technocratization of interpersonal relations with the same conviction they support the mystery of committed love. Everywhere, they will prefer subtlety to panacea, diversity to uniformity, mutuality to competition and interdependence to separatism. They will, in other words, be deeply and radically subversive of western society's institutionalized decadence, not by echoing the fashionable scientistic iconoclasm that in fact is integral to the civilization it pretends to assail, but by insisting that no civilization can survive, no polity remain free and just, unless the human trinity of woman, man and child sanctifies its spirit.

I have no doubt that such a program of reform will, because it is more arduous, less facile, and in a sense more profoundly radical than so many fashionable schemes for human liberation, be looked upon with doubt and skepticism. The alternatives come easier. To excoriate marriage is inviting; it is almost dead anyway. To censure men takes little courage; they are for the most part more confused and impotent and ridden with despair than women. To polarize nature and liberty makes a certain sense; neither have to be taken seriously. To challenge the ethos of our civilization is far more difficult, far less certain of success. Raising standards renders the standard-bearer vulnerable. The road to polity is tortuous and the signposts have disappeared. Narcissism, technocracy, uniformity, simple-mindedness, skepticism, competition, acquisitivenss, impotence and despair are degenerative diseases of advanced cultures that no society has previously cured—that few have ever faced. To ask that women preoccupied with their condition and men who think women's cause just, concern themselves with so formidable a challenge is to ask a great deal. Yet if our interest is truly that elusive liberation after which women have named their move-

ment, we have no choice but to ask that of ourselves.
Jean-Jacques Rousseau, sexist that he was, understood it
perfectly:

> Liberty is a food easy to eat, but hard to digest; it takes
> very strong stomachs to stand it. I laugh at those debased
> peoples who, allowing themselves to be stirred up by re-
> bels, dare to speak of liberty without having the slightest
> idea of its meaning, and who imagine that, in order to be
> free, it is enough to be insubordinate. O proud and holy
> liberty! If those poor people could only know thee, if they
> realized at what a price thou art won and preserved; if
> they felt how much more austere are thy laws than the
> yoke of tyrants is heavy: their feeble souls would fear thee
> a hundred times more than slavery; they would flee from
> thee in terror, as from a burden threatening to crush
> them.

Women and men shall know this liberty together—
secured by mutual struggle, sustained by mutual love—
or they shall never know it at all.

Bibliography

Adorno, Theodor et al. *The Authoritarian Personality.* New York: Harper & Row, 1950.

Ardrey, Robert. *African Genesis.* New York: Atheneum, 1961.

———. *The Territorial Imperative.* New York: Atheneum, 1966.

Aristotle. *The Politics.* Translated by Ernest Barker. Oxford: Oxford University Press, 1946.

Beauvoir, Simone de. *The Second Sex.* New York: Alfred A. Knopf, 1953.

Bengis, Ingrid. *Combat in the Erogenous Zone.* New York: Alfred A. Knopf, 1972.

Bettelheim, Bruno. *Children of the Dream.* New York: Macmillan, 1969.

Cooper, David. *The Death of the Family.* New York: Random House, 1971.

Darwin, Charles. *On the Origin of Species.* London: John Murray, 1859.

Davis, Elizabeth Gould. *The First Sex.* New York: G.P. Putnam's Sons, 1971.

Dechter, Midge. *The New Chastity and Other Arguments Against*

Woman's Liberation. New York: Coward, McCann & Geoghegan, 1972.

Engels, Frederick. *The Origin of the Family, Private Property and the State* (1884), and *Socialism: Scientific and Utopian* (1892). In Marx and Engels. *Selected Works in Two Volumes.* Moscow: Foreign Languages Publishing House, 1951.

Erikson, Erik. *Childhood and Society.* New York: W. W. Norton, 1950.————. *Identity: Youth and Crisis.* New York: W.W. Norton, 1968

Firestone, Shulamith. *The Dialectic of Sex.* New York: William Morrow, 1970.

Friedan, Betty. *The Feminine Mystique.* New York: W.W. Norton, 1963.

————. "Up From the Kitchen Floor." *The New York Times Magazine,* March 4, 1973.

Freud, Sigmund. *Civilization and Its Discontents.* Translated by Joan Riviere. Garden City, N.Y.: Doubleday, 1958.

Fromm, Erich. *Escape From Freedom.* New York: Holt, Rinehart and Winston, 1941.

Gilder, George. *Sexual Suicide.* New York: Quadrangle Books, 1973.

Goldberg, Steven. *The Inevitability of Patriarchy.* New York: William Morrow, 1973.

Greer, Germaine. *The Female Eunuch.* New York: McGraw-Hill, 1971.

Hegel, G.W.F. *The Philosophy of History.* Translated by G. Sibree. The Colonial Press, 1899.

Heilbrun, Carolyn G. *Towards a Recognition of Androgyny.* New York: Alfred A. Knopf, 1973.

Hobbes, Thomas. *The Leviathan.* London, 1651.

Hollander, Xaviera. *The Happy Hooker.* New York: Dell, 1972.

Jaffe, Rona. "Listening In On New York's Elite Teenagers." *New York Magazine,* May 15, 1972.

Johnston, Jill. *Lesbian Nation.* New York: Simon & Schuster, 1973.

———. "Lesbian Mothers ltd." *The Village Voice,* March 9, 1972.

Jong, Erica. *Fear of Flying.* New York: Holt, Rinehart and Winston, 1973.

Katz, Elia. *Armed Love.* New York: Holt, Rinehart and Winston, 1971.

Koedt, Anne. "The Myth of Vaginal Orgasm" in *Radical Feminism* (Anne Koedt, ed.) New York: Quadrangle Books, 1972.

Kropotkin, Prince Petr Alekseevich. *Mutual Aid.* Boston: Extending Horizon Books, n.d.

Laing, R. D. *The Divided Self.* London: Tavistock Publications, 1960.

LaRue, Linda J. M. "Black Liberation and Women's Lib." *Trans-Action,* November-December, 1970.

Locke, John. *The Second Treatise of Civil Government.* London, 1698.

Lorenz, Konrad. *On Aggression.* New York: Harcourt, Brace & World, 1966.

Mailer, Norman. *The Prisoner of Sex.* Boston: Little, Brown, 1971.

Maine, Sir Henry. *Ancient Law.* London, 1861.

Marx, Karl. *The Communist Manifesto* (1848). In *Marx and Engels: The Selected Works.* Moscow: Foreign Languages Publishing House, 1951.

Masters, W.H. and Johnson, V.E. with Levin, R.J. *The Pleasure Bond.* Boston: Little, Brown, 1975.

McWilliams, Wilson Carey. *The Idea of Fraternity in America.* Berkeley: University of California Press, 1973.

Mead, Margaret. *Male and Female: A Study of the Sexes in a Changing World.* New York: William Morrow, 1949.

Mill, John Stuart. *The Subjection of Women*. London: Longman's, 1869.

Millet, Kate. *Sexual Politics*. Garden City, N. Y.: Doubleday, 1970.

Mitchell, Juliet. *Woman's Estate*. New York: Pantheon, 1971.

————. *Psychoanalysis and Feminism*. London: Allen Lane, 1974.

Montagu, Ashley. *The Natural Superiority of Women*, Third Revised Edition. New York: Random House, 1974.

Morgan, Elaine. *The Descent of Women*. New York: Stein & Day, 1972.

Morgan, Robin (ed.). *Sisterhood is Powerful: An Anthology*. New York: Random House, 1970.

Morris, Desmond. *The Naked Ape*. New York: McGraw-Hill, 1968.

Nisbet, Robert. *The Quest for Community*. Oxford: Oxford University Press, 1953.

O'Neill, Nena and George. *Open Marriage*. New York: Avon, 1973.

Peck, Ellen. *The Baby Trap*. New York: Bernard Geis, 1971.

Perutz, Kathrin. *Marriage Is Hell*. New York: William Morrow, 1972.

Plath, Sylvia. *The Bell Jar*. New York: Harper & Row, 1971.

Plato. *The Republic*. Translated by F.M. Cornford. Oxford: Oxford University Press, 1941.

Proudhon, P.J. *Selected Writings*. Garden City, New York: Doubleday, 1969.

Reich, Charles. *The Greening of America*. New York: Random House, 1970.

Reyburn, Wallace. *The Inferior Sex*. Englewood Cliffs, N. J.: Prentice-Hall, 1972.

Rousseau, Jean-Jacques. *The Social Contract*. London: Everyman, 1913.

————. *Emile*. London: Everyman, 1911.

Sagan, Françoise. *Scars on the Soul*. New York: McGraw-Hill, 1974.

Sherfey, Mary Jane. *The Nature and Evolution of Female Sexuality*. New York: Random House, 1972.

Skinner, B. F. *Beyond Freedom and Dignity*. New York: Alfred A. Knopf, 1971.

Slater, Philip. *Earthwalk*. Garden City, N.Y.: Doubleday, 1974.

Terkel, Studs. *Working*. New York: Pantheon, 1974.

Tiger, Lionel. *Men in Groups*. New York: Random House, 1969.

————. "Male Dominance? Yes, Alas. A Sexist Plot? No." *The New York Times Magazine*. October 25, 1970.

Tiger, Lionel and Fox, Robin. *The Imperial Animal*. New York: Holt, Rinehart and Winston, 1971.

Tönnies, Ferdinand. *Community and Society*. East Lansing, Michigan: Michigan State University Press, 1957.

Vilar, Esther. *The Manipulated Man*. New York: Farrar, Strauss and Giroux, 1972.

Walker, Nancy. *The Life Swap*. New York: Dial Press, 1974.